The Great American Staycation

a Garden A Day at the Beach Arts & Crafts Movie Night CAMP AT HOME

The Great American Staycation

How to Make a **Vacation at Home** Fun for the Whole Family

(and your wallet!)

Adamsmedia

Avon, Massachusetts

Balloon Ride Go Sailing Matt Wixon HOMEGAME Cheer the Home Team Theme Park Fun!

Published by
Adams Media, a division of F+W Media, Inc.
57 Littlefield Street, Avon, MA 02322. U.S.A.
www.adamsmedia.com

ISBN 10: 1-60550-656-7
ISBN 13: 978-1-60550-656-2

Printed in the United States of America.

J I H G F E D C B A

Library of Congress Cataloging-in-Publication Data
is available from the publisher.

This publication is designed to provide accurate and authoritative information with
regard to the subject matter covered. It is sold with the understanding that the publisher is not engaged in rendering legal, accounting, or other professional advice. If
legal advice or other expert assistance is required, the services of a competent professional person should be sought.

—From a *Declaration of Principles* jointly adopted by a Committee of the
American Bar Association and a Committee of Publishers and Associations

Many of the designations used by manufacturers and sellers to distinguish their product are claimed as trademarks. Where those designations appear in this book and
Adams Media was aware of a trademark claim, the designations have been printed with
initial capital letters.

This book is available at quantity discounts for bulk purchases.
For information, please call 1-800-289-0963.

For Janell and my three biggest motivators—Ryan, Cooper, and Nathan.

Acknowledgments

Thanks to Amy and Kevin, Andy, Brenda and Ed, Brian, Carrie, Cristi, D. Ray, Joslyn, Katie and Chris, Lin, Melissa, Nancy B., Nancy and Mike Z., Nikki and Donald, Norma, Tom, Toni, and everyone else who shared their ideas and experiences. I hope your next staycation is fun, memorable, and doesn't include a writer bugging you about the details.

Contents

Chapter 2

Staycation Rules

9

Chapter 3
Theme Parks and Thrill Rides
25

Chapter 4

Outdoors and Adventure

39

Chapter 5

Educational Staycations

53

Chapter 6

The Pampered Life

73

Chapter 7

Sports Staycations

85

Chapter 8

Movies, Plays, and Other Entertainment

99

Chapter 9

Romantic Staycations

115

Chapter 10

Especially for Kids

129

Chapter 11

Some More Ways to Pack in Fun

149

Chapter 12

Making the Most of It

167

Introduction

Twenty-five years before *staycation* became a buzzword, my parents packed their three kids into a rented van for an overnight "fake-cation."

Yes, a fake-cation. As in *fake vacation*.

After all, the van wasn't really rented. My parents got it at a reduced rate, or maybe even free, in exchange for listening to a sales pitch on conversion vans. When the sales pitch was over, the van was all ours for the next twenty-four hours.

And what a twenty-four hours it was!

To escape the summer heat in Phoenix, Arizona, we drove seventy-five miles north to higher elevation. We swam in a creek, ate dinner somewhere, and then slept in the van in a grocery store parking lot. One bench seat folded flat into a bed, and my parents slept there. My brother slept on the floor, and my sister and I each slept in a captain's chair.

The captain's chairs reclined less than an airplane seat, making sleep almost impossible. I remember struggling to get comfortable as I watched cars zoom by on a freeway next to us. The next morning, with our twenty-four hours nearly complete, we headed home.

It was one of several fake-cations my family took when I was a kid. One time we spent a weekend in a townhouse that required my parents to sit through a three-hour sales pitch.

Another time, our family spent a weekend at an RV park that was mostly populated by retirees. The park had a small, deteriorating miniature golf course that was fun for an hour or two. But after that, my brother, sister, and I had nothing to do but play cards in the RV and walk over to the shuffleboard courts and sling around the sliding disks. I remember I ate an entire box of Cheez-Its in one day during that trip. Not because I was hungry, just because it was something to pass the time. The most memorable moment of that weekend was when my brother and I, tired of watching the three channels available on our portable five-inch, black-and-white TV, walked to the RV park's community center. There we found a television set to watch, but that only lasted a few minutes. We got yelled at for turning up the volume because it was interfering with the man calling out the bingo numbers.

Very memorable, but not the greatest vacation. Truly a fake-cation.

But I don't blame my parents. Three kids were expensive to fly anywhere. And the emotional cost was probably higher, given that my brother, sister, and I could get into an argument in the middle of church. On Christmas Eve.

Money was tight, and so was time. My dad, an insurance salesman, switched companies so often that he didn't accumulate a lot of vacation days. He did accumulate a lot of business cards, however, and we used the backs of the outdated ones to write down phone messages.

Obviously, the seven-day family vacation to Walt Disney World wasn't an option for my family. But now that I've taken some jabs at my parents, I'll give them some credit. Even without much money or time, they still wanted to put some kind of vacation together.

That's exactly what millions of Americans, including me, are thinking right now. How are we going to spend our next vacation?

We'd all love to really splurge. We'd love to jet away for a fourteen-day trip to somewhere exotic. We'd love to lounge on an exclusive beach and snap our fingers to have someone deliver us food, drinks, and in my case, SPF 140 sunblock. But for many of us, reality cramps our vacation fantasies. The economy is in a downturn; gas prices are up and down (but usually up); and airlines are cutting flights, hiking fares, and adding fees for checking luggage. They're even charging for pillows now. Eventually, I'm guessing the airlines will add a "passenger convenience fee" to any flight that doesn't end with an exit by inflatable slide.

The airlines are a little desperate, obviously. And there's a good reason why. In June of 2008, consumer confidence hit its lowest level in sixteen years. Inflation is up, home values are sinking, and salaries are stagnant.

In an Associated Press story that was printed in newspapers across the country, an economist described it this way: "From a consumer perspective, this is the most troubling economy since the 1980s."

Economic conditions are painful, no doubt. So what do we have to do? Unfortunately, as much as we hate it in this country of big hopes, big dreams, and Big Macs, it's time to downsize.

That brings us to the staycation. The stay-at-home vacation. The kind of vacation nobody really talked about until it became a product of necessity. The kind of vacation that my parents tried to pull off back when the economy was in another mighty swan dive.

But those were fake-cations. A staycation doesn't have to be that way.

I know this because I'm now in the position my parents were in twenty-five years ago. Like my parents, my wife and I have three kids. And since we started having our kids, and heard "it's a boy!" three times, we've spent many vacations at home.

Finances are a big reason. It's expensive to take kids on vacation, and after our first son was born six years ago, my wife suspended her career as a teacher. Another reason we started taking staycations, although we never called them that, was just how stressful it is to travel with kids.

When we fly, I feel like I'm toting an entire section of Babies 'R Us onto a plane. It's just like every time I go to the neighborhood pool with the kids. Let's see. Do we have everything? Towels, boogie board, pool noodle float thing, hats, goggles, swim shoes, water guns, two cups of water, Spider-Man dive toy . . . yes, we've got everything. Loaded down with all that stuff, I waddle along behind the kids as we walk to the pool. Now I know how my wife felt when she was pregnant.

Wait, no, I don't. She might read this. Hey, can we erase that last sentence?

Anyway, my wife and I and our kids have taken a lot of staycations. Some great, some not-so-great. But it all leads up to this:

The only thing I know about the future is that it's uncertain. Even if my sons manage to stay out of emergency rooms, big expenses lie ahead. Greater financial challenges, too. So if I can save some money now, I'm better prepared for the future. A staycation will help me do that.

I've learned a lot over the years about how to have a good, and bad, staycation. In the chapters that follow, I'll pass along some tips, strategies, and ideas for making it a good one. Some will be simple, some more elaborate, some dirt cheap, and some that, at least for a staycation, might be considered extravagant.

Some ideas won't be new to you. Others might lead you to wonder why you didn't think of it yourself. And one or two might lead you to say, "That seems a little crazy."

If that happens, remember two things:

1. A staycation is most successful when you have a positive attitude and willingness to adjust the traditional notion of what a vacation is.
2. This book was written by a guy who once ran into a parked car while playing street football. I may have suffered permanent damage. Or perhaps I was damaged beforehand.

The ideas in the book should help you plan your next staycation. Whether you're single, a couple, or a couple and more, you will find something that fits. But this book will have more than ideas for your staycation. I also want it to be a source of encouragement as you plan your vacation time. So what if you're spending an evening at the community theater instead of seeing *The Phantom of the Opera* on Broadway. You can still make it special.

And don't be embarrassed that you're taking a staycation. Just about everyone in the country is feeling the pinch, and staycations are a way for individuals, couples, and families to get away from it all without breaking the bank.

Throughout the book, my fellow staycationers will tell their stories. They'll talk about their favorite ideas, what worked well and sometimes not so well, and their keys to a successful staycation. I'll also share some of my experiences in travel, as a kid, and as a dad with kids.

So let's get started. When you're finished, I hope you'll be ready to plan a staycation that doesn't feel like a fake-cation. You can make it real, you can make it special, and you can make it memorable.

Memorable for the right reasons, I mean. Because I'll never forget that night I spent sitting in the conversion van, trying to fall asleep, staring at a glowing McDonald's sign.

Chapter 1
What Is a Staycation? And How Can It Work for You?

According to *Urban Dictionary*, a *staycation* is "A vacation that is spent at one's home enjoying all that home and one's home environs have to offer."

That definition seems about right. Spending a vacation at home or close to home. But the best way to define a staycation, at least for this book, is this way:

> *A vacation in which the vacationer stays at home, or near home, while creating the environment of a traditional vacation.*

What does "creating the environment of a traditional vacation" mean? That's probably the most important part of the definition. But first, let's get some specifics out of the way.

The Magic Number Is 100

This book will consider "near home" any location within about 100 miles. That's because a 200-mile round trip seems to be a reasonable upper limit for a destination that can be traveled to and enjoyed in one day. Unless you routinely drive at more than 100 miles per hour, in which case you should proceed directly to the chapter on thrill rides. Or to jail.

You can, of course, travel farther than 100 miles for a staycation activity. The perfect camping spot might be 125 miles away or a great amusement park might mean a 150-mile drive. In that case, my rule is more of a guideline. But if you need a full tank of gas just to get somewhere, that's pushing it.

Before you start on a long drive, look for attractions nearby the way staycationer Lin B. did. The increased prices for gasoline and airline tickets were the big reasons she and her husband stayed close to home, but seeing all the tourists in her hometown made the decision easier.

"Here we are living in the Dallas–Fort Worth area and have never been to any of the museums, water parks, theme parks, and other local attractions that so many out-of-towners come to see," Lin said.

"It was like a light bulb went off in our minds at the same time, when we suddenly realized we'd always taken vacations to get out of town and out-of-towners were leaving their own hometowns to come here."

Close to Home, but Light-Years Away

Maybe the light bulb will go off for you, too. Or maybe you still really want to get out of town but have no choice. Either way, the important thing is to make your staycation the best it can be.

To do that, you need to create the environment of a traditional vacation. But what does that mean?

It's pretty simple, really. It means getting out of the rut of your daily life. It means not planning a stay-at-home vacation that combines leisure time with cleaning out the garage, building bookshelves, and a trip to get the car repaired. That's not a vacation at all.

People have been spending their vacation days that way for years. Every now and then you need a few vacation days just to catch up on everything, or at least not fall further behind. I guess you could call that an "efficiency vacation," but it's probably better not to call it a vacation at all.

Some people would say the same about a staycation. After all, the traditional notion of a vacation includes traveling somewhere far away. A vacation means you take a flight, or a long car ride with a hotel stay, and arrive at a vacation destination. Getting away from it all means, in a physical way, getting away from it all.

Hassle-Free Fun

There's a lot of value to that. A traditional vacation creates a tangible break from the daily grind. It whisks you away from the everyday and takes you out of your stressful environment. Unfortunately, it also throws you into an environment that includes crowded airports, delayed flights, and the technological marvel of body-scanning machines that look under clothes and really get to know you.

And if you're traveling with kids?

Well, humorist Robert Benchley put it this way:

"Traveling with children corresponds roughly to traveling third class in Bulgaria."

Benchley died in 1945, but his observation about traveling with kids holds up. I've never traveled any class to Bulgaria, but I have walked down the aisle of an airplane with a baby car seat and watched passengers attempt to telepathically block me from taking the seat next to them.

Many other perils and peeves await today's traveler, so for some people, the staycation isn't a completely financial decision. You've probably heard someone return from vacation and say they need a vacation to recover from a vacation.

That person could be Nancy B., who enjoys taking staycations with her husband.

"When we work all week, an ideal vacation is to just stay at home and enjoy the fruits of our labors from the long hours at the office," she said. "We have never fallen victim to the usual 'tourist traps' anyhow and prefer to find or make our own fun."

Another staycationer, Katie H., weighs in:

"Those that think the only definition of vacation is flying across the world to sip margaritas on some foreign beach are in dire need of a reality check," said Katie, who likes to staycation with her husband, Chris, in northern California. "Those who don't like to stay home and need to be busy should consider that there is plenty to do in the local area."

Katie and Chris did take a trip to Hawaii a few years ago and stayed in a five-diamond resort. It was wonderful, she said, and—this was the most important part—all expenses paid. But as for other traditional vacations. . . .

"We don't feel that making a trip somewhere that involves an airplane ride, rental car, hotel, and massive credit card bills after the fact sounds that appealing."

Yes, the traditional vacation can be tiring. And frustrating. And include your suitcase doing loops in a London baggage claim as you land in Cairo. But I'm not going to sugarcoat this book with an idea that a staycation is better than a traditional vacation. I know that a staycation is a product of necessity and that most people would prefer to take a traditional vacation. It's just that economic conditions have put the squeeze on their plans.

How can you tell if a staycation is right for you? It might depend on which of the following statements are most likely to come from you:

IS A STAYCATION RIGHT FOR YOU?

Yes, a staycation is right for you.	*No, probably not.*
The best part of a vacation is the time spent with family and friends.	The best part of a vacation is getting out of this godforsaken place I live in.
A vacation isn't a vacation if it doesn't get me away from my everyday life, help me relax, and refresh me for my return to work.	A vacation isn't a vacation if it doesn't include bringing my toothbrush, packing at least three pairs of underwear, and hearing a flight attendant say "full-and-upright position."
If I don't take a vacation that includes a flight or a long road trip, I will save money.	If I don't take a vacation that includes a flight or a long road trip, the terrorists will have won.
The glass is half full.	The glass is half empty.
There are many attractions in my hometown that I have not visited.	There are many attractions in my hometown that I have not visited, but I still can't get out of this godforsaken place fast enough.

A lot of cities began trying to capitalize on the staycation trend in the summer of 2008. New York City began marketing "Go Local" to its citizens to keep their tourist dollars in the city and help replace the dollars lost when out-of-town tourists opted for staycations. The convention and visitors bureau in Arlington, Texas, dedicated a section of its website to staycations with the slogan, "Stay close to home. Stay close to fun." And the state of Washington's tourism website greeted visitors with this:

"Who says you need to travel far from home for this year's summer vacation? You can find plenty of amazing Washington experiences in your own backyard."

That's probably true for wherever you live. Regardless of how you came to the decision to take a staycation, you can probably find amazing experiences in your own backyard. But for people still smarting from watching vacation plans vaporize as the economy stumbles and travel costs shoot up, adapting to the staycation idea might not be easy. At least at first.

"It's a rite of passage in America to say, 'I went on a big vacation,'" said Joslyn T., a mother of two who has taken several staycations. "But right now, it makes sense to stay home."

Yes it does. But it doesn't mean you have to give up your vacation. A staycation can be a real vacation. Once again, this book's definition:

A vacation in which the vacationer stays at home, or near home, while creating the environment of a traditional vacation.

Make It Your Own

Our definition of staycation is pretty broad, but so is each person's definition of a traditional vacation. For some people, the perfect vacation means glacier hiking in Alaska or kayaking on the Colorado River through the Grand Canyon. Others would prefer a place such as Walt Disney World, New York City, or just a beach where they can turn off their cell phone and read a book.

The same is true for a staycation. Depending on what's right for you, and your budget, your staycation might be spent mostly inside your house. It might also include a day cruise, a two-day stay at a nearby resort, a concert, a museum visit, tickets to the theater, or a day of thrill rides at an amusement park.

Or it could include all of those activities in one week. You might even be able to throw in a hot air balloon ride. You can do that with a staycation, and when it's over, well. . . .

Brian W., who takes a traditional vacation each year and spends another one at home, says it best:

"You don't leave your staycation more tired than you did going into it."

Chapter 2
Staycation Rules

Off you go on an unforgettable seven-day family cruise to the Caribbean. You've got the camera, the sunscreen, calypso music on the iPod, and a vacation vibe so intense that you're actually considering getting your blonde hair braided in cornrows. You are *so* ready for a vacation.

And then on the first day, your five-year-old says the boat makes his tummy feel funny. On day two, he doesn't want anything from the buffet. On day three, as you lounge on the deck, feeling the wind tickle your developing sunburn, a cruise worker runs to you and says, "Please come quickly! Your son just threw up during the treasure hunt at Camp Adventure Kids."

At that moment, and during the rest of your trip with a child who proves not to be seaworthy, a staycation sounds fantastic. But that's not why I started the chapter on staycation rules with a tale of high distress on the high seas.

Here's the reason: The way seasickness can doom a cruise is exactly how breaking the staycation rules can doom a less exotic vacation.

Wait. There are rules for a staycation?

Yes, there are.

Rules might seem out of place when talking about a vacation. After all, a vacation is supposed be a break from the rules, responsibilities, and schedules that govern our lives. But these are rules that will help you do that.

Especially *Staycation Rule #1,* which trumps all other rules.

Rule #1: A Staycation Must Be Treated as a Real Vacation

Rule #1 means that just because you're not getting on that cruise trip, you still need to do the same mental checkout of the real world that typical vacations entail. That means turning off your cell phone and not checking your e-mail each day. It means getting all the household chores done before the start of your staycation. It means not thinking, "If we leave the show just before the curtain falls, then we can beat traffic, I'll be in bed before midnight, and can get up early tomorrow to mow the lawn."

For any vacation, a staycation or something grander, you have to unplug. Unplug from work, from your chores, from the daily compulsion to get things done. Nancy and Mike Z., a couple in Massachusetts with three kids under four years old, decided this before their staycation.

"We went into it with the mindset that we were not going to do much with the house, it wasn't going to be one of these times when we're off work and we have to get this done and we have to get that done," Nancy said. "That mindset made it feel worthwhile so it still felt like a vacation."

Exactly. But if spending your vacation working on household projects makes you happy, then do it. If you're content with filling your vacation with cleaning the house, reviewing your investment portfolio, and a checkup at the dentist, that's okay, too.

For a satisfying staycation, however, or at least one that in some way resembles a traditional vacation, you have to let go. Joslyn T. told of a family she knew that—long before *staycation* became a buzzword—would treat their staycations with the "reverence of a regular vacation."

The mother, father, and their two teenagers would have a family meeting before the staycation began and set the ground rules for how they would spend their time together. They recorded an answering machine message to tell callers to call back after their vacation was over.

During the family meeting, each day of the staycation was also planned. That leads to the next rule.

Rule #2: Plan Ahead

Remember the classic movie, *National Lampoon's Vacation?* It featured Chevy Chase as the overly enthusiastic, dimwitted Clark Griswold taking his family on a road trip that included asking for directions in a rough part of town, getting ripped off by mechanics, and visiting hick relatives who stirred Kool-Aid with their hands.

But it all seemed worth it when the Griswold family reached its destination, Wally World. Unfortunately, when Clark and his family got to the entrance, a statue of Marty Moose announced:

"Sorry, folks! We're closed for two weeks to clean and repair America's favorite family fun park."

Clark still got his family into the park by buying a BB gun and kidnapping a security guard, but you probably don't want to go that far. Plan ahead and you won't be disappointed, embarrassed in front of your kids, or led away in handcuffs.

For example, many art museums are closed on Mondays and so are some restaurants. Factory tours, which are a fun idea discussed later, usually aren't available every day. Same goes for a sunset cruise you want to take. If you want to attend some sporting events during your staycation, and then realize too late that the team is on a two-week road trip, you're out of luck.

As with any vacation, if you wing it, you're probably going to fly into a wall. So do some research on the Internet, buy tickets ahead of time, and find out what you can and can't do.

Before the vacation begins, have each member of the family make a list of what he or she wants to do during the staycation. Then sketch out what you want to do on each of your vacation days. That allows you to prioritize and see how everything will fit together. You can always make changes later.

Planning was important to staycationers Tom and Laura M., empty-nesters in Florida, whose second attempt at a staycation went well. But the first one a year earlier was a bit of a disaster.

"We didn't have anything planned, and it didn't turn out that well," Tom said. "There were a lot of dead spots and a lot of bored spots."

So before the second staycation, Tom and Laura made lists of what they wanted to do, combined them, and made some compromises. They ended up cooking new foods at home, including what Tom called "off-the-wall exotic stuff." They had picnics at a local park, swam in their backyard pool, and got books and movies at the library.

"A huge success," Tom said.

Rule #3: Choose a Start and End Date

The best staycations should feel like a real vacation. So like a real vacation, give your staycation specific start and end dates.

Before the start date, mow the lawn, take care of that rattling sound in the car's engine, clean the house, and pay the bills that will be due during your time off. Take care of any household projects that, if left unfinished, will restrict you during your staycation. You can even tell friends and family that you won't be taking calls during your staycation or record a message for the answering machine. (On the message, specifically say it's a staycation and not a vacation because you don't want to be a target for burglars.)

If you're spending most of the staycation in your home, consider hiring maid service for one week. At the very least, put off as much housework as possible. This is supposed to be a time when you get away from the everyday chores, activities, and worries.

If even the smallest messes in your house stress you out, then go ahead and do some housework. But if you can't go a week without cleaning the baseboards or washing windows, you don't need a staycation, you need an intervention.

Rule #4: Create Mental Distance

The goal with any vacation is to leave the worn path of everyday life. A traditional vacation achieves that with a physical distance between you and your day-to-day world. But with a staycation, you need to create a mental distance.

How do you do that?

One way is by resisting the urge to be productive, which isn't easy to do in our busy lives. Workloads are heavy, free time is limited, and efficiency is valued. We're told to make the most of every moment.

Well, you should make the most of every moment of your staycation. That's why you shouldn't feel, just because you're staying home, that you need to get things done around the house. Turn off your mobile phone, stay away from your work e-mail account, and if you have a home office, throw a blanket over the computer. Whatever you need to do to break away from the compulsion to get things done.

Be strong. It's tempting to give in to the excitement of replacing the caulk around a shower or powerwash the fence (sarcasm alert), but try to keep yourself away. A lineup of household projects is a staycation killer.

Another way to create mental distance is by deliberately changing things up for a week or two. Try staying up late and sleeping later. Eat at different times and eat different foods. Eat breakfast for dinner and dinner for breakfast. Go somewhere in your city, or a nearby city, where you've never been. And try one activity or type of entertainment that you've never tried.

"My favorite part is getting away from work and our usual life. It's nice to break the [kids'] routine of get up, turn on Nick TV, eat cereal, loll around for six hours, take a nap," said staycationer Carrie S.

Day trips are a big part of staycations for Carrie and her husband. So is a willingness to try something different.

"If we've gone somewhere away from home," Carrie said, "we find something to do that's specific to where we are, trying hard not do what we could be doing at home."

Simple changes made a difference for Katie and Chris during their staycation in California. Instead of driving to the gym in a hurry, they were able to take their time and walk the half mile there.

"Instead of driving everywhere, we biked and got to see things that we usually fly by and take for granted," Katie said. "I appreciated being able to take time and be an active participant in my life."

Rule #5: Treat Yourself

Your reason for a staycation is probably budget-related, but it still needs to be a vacation. You don't have to be frivolous, but don't skimp, either. You'll still save money.

That's why you should eat at restaurants as often as possible during your staycation. Your budget might determine how frequently and where you do this, but grocery shopping, fixing a meal, cleaning up the table, and doing the dishes is a big part of the daily grind. Of course, if you enjoy cooking, a staycation is a great time to indulge in it. Try new recipes, try new styles of food, and if you're pretty good at it, try to make it to my house during your staycation. Anyone who wants to cook is always welcome.

As for eating out, it doesn't have to be fine dining. It can be hitting a sandwich shop for lunch and an inexpensive casual restaurant for dinner. Any place where you can relax for a few minutes and leave the dirty dishes when you're finished will do the trick.

Treating yourself also means staying away from diet foods. In fact, don't even think about a diet during your staycation. After all, eating without guilt is part of the fun of a vacation. Imagine going on a cruise where you're surrounded by fine dining, twenty-four-hour bistros, and those midnight buffets so elaborate that cruisers take photographs of the spread before eating. The food is one of the highlights. If you stayed true to your diet, it would be more like torture than fun.

The same will happen on your staycation. Dieting is good for your health, and it has helped me maintain washboard abs for years (lie alert). But dieting is a sacrifice, and you don't need another reason to consider your staycation a sacrifice.

That should be true for everything you do. You are, of course, making a sacrifice by staying at home for your vacation. But that should give you some license to splurge. You'll find lots of ways to do that in the chapters that follow.

Rule #6: Remember It

My parents didn't embrace technology. Although camcorders were around during my childhood in the 1980s, most of the video of my adolescence is on filmstrips. My parents' outdated camera had no zoom, no sound, and indoor filming required a light that could burn retinas.

In every video, family members waved frantically at the camera to compensate for the lack of sound. Occasionally, someone would try to mouth some words. In the final years of the silent era, when the teenage kids were allowed to operate the outdated technology, our creativity bubbled over into writing words in the dirt with a stick.

Pretty sad, huh?

But here's the thing. We still loved to watch the videos, and watching them today brings back great memories. So, too, will the photos and videos you take during your staycation, even if it's not the vacation of your dreams. It's easy to forget about taking pictures and shooting video when you don't take a traditional vacation, so make a point of taking photos and/or video each day. It's also part of creating the mental distance from your daily routine.

Buy souvenirs, too. If you visit a wax museum, bring something home from the gift shop. If you spend some time at a water park, buy one of those commemorative water bottles that are too tall for the dishwasher. If you go camping, keep the empty bottle of calamine lotion to remember your encounter with poison ivy.

Just kidding about the last one. But do buy souvenirs. You can also make them, which we'll talk about more in the "Especially for Kids" chapter.

Rule #7: Maximize Your Hometown

My wife and I have lived in the Dallas area for nearly ten years, but until we had kids and started spending some vacations in town, I had no idea how much was offered nearby. Friends and family would come to visit, ask me what places they should check out, and this was my response: "There's the Sixth Floor Museum, which has everything about the JFK assassination, and Southfork Ranch, where *Dallas* was filmed."

Both are great to visit. The Sixth Floor Museum for the history; Southfork Ranch for a reminder of how much hairspray can actually be used on one head. But now I know I could've directed my friends to dozens of other places: museums, entertainment districts, wildlife centers, historic neighborhoods, amusement parks, even a place not far away that has life-size dinosaur sculptures and footprints left by dinosaurs 100 million years ago.

You'll find some of the same gems in your hometown or nearby: places you don't think of exploring, or don't have the time to, during your standard workweek. Katie and Chris made that a big part of their staycation.

"We acted like tourists in our own town, going to historical places, state parks, and other places we've always wanted to visit," Katie said. "My camera hung from my neck screamed 'tourist!' but we loved every minute of it and got to know our town a whole lot better."

So how do you find these historical places, state parks, and other attractions? One easy way is to contact your city's department of tourism or visitors' bureau. They are usually easy to find on a city government's website. Also ask the visitors' bureau about discount tickets for local attractions. If the out-of-towners are getting a special rate, you should, too.

An even easier way to find local attractions is to stop by the lobby of a nearby hotel. Attractions within driving distance will have their brochures on display there. If the hotel's desk clerk asks what you're doing, just say you're a local exploring your hometown.

Or you can speak English in a German accent and act like you're lost.

Rule #8: Stay Positive

The staycation isn't the Hawaiian vacation or two weeks in Paris that you really wanted to take this year. Fine, that's disappointing. But dwell on that and your staycation will undoubtedly be a disaster. You'll take another big vacation one day, but for now, focus on what you can do.

Attitude is "150 percent important," said Carrie S. "You have to acknowledge that this isn't the trip of a lifetime, but it is an opportunity to do something that you may not have done before. It's about being together as a family, or a couple, or whatever you are, and being away from work, school, other things that interfere. Focus on one another, and the other perks of the trip are just that: perks."

Again, focus on what you can do. Also consider that according to the United States Bureau of Labor Statistics, about a quarter of all workers in the private sector receive *zero* paid vacation. It's true. A quarter of workers get nothing but weekends and holidays to cut loose. For all the paid vacationers reading this, that's at least one reason to raise a half-full glass to your experiment in staycationing.

So let's get going. Oh yeah, and here's one last thing to remember. It's from William Doherty, a professor of family social science at the University of Minnesota. In a *New York Times* article, here was his quote:

"Vacations tend to create memories more than any other family activity, and the bad times are some of the best memories."

The bad times are some of the best memories. That must be why I so vividly remember trying to sleep sitting up in the conversion van and the time when my dad didn't see the "low clearance" sign and scraped up the top of the rented RV. Or the time on vacation when our family car wouldn't stop running even after the key was taken out of the ignition.

Anyway, take what the professor said as words of encouragement. Even if your staycation plans jump the tracks, you'll be creating memories that help you bond with your family, friends, or whoever joins you on your "Greetings from Nearby!" adventure.

How This Book Is Organized

The staycation ideas that follow are organized in chapters that fit a particular type of traditional vacation, but it's not a perfect way to do it because a staycation, like any vacation, doesn't have to fit into any category.

Three days of outdoors and adventure followed by a three-day movie marathon might be just the right mix for one person. A day of thrill rides followed by a few days of spa-like pampering might appeal to another. Others might want to be very low key and rarely set foot outside their front door. They, too, will be able to find ideas here for their staycation. There's not a chapter titled "Never Leaving Your Home," but ideas from each chapter will apply.

Each chapter will also include online resources to help you research and plan your staycation. I included them in the text of the chapter and also listed all the links in the "Help on the Net" section at the end of the chapter, along with some extra links.

The right attitude is also essential to a staycation. So to help you stay positive, throughout this book the "Staycation Bonus" boxes will point out the negatives of a traditional vacation. These are the little aspects of traveling that—although we all still want to take the big, exciting trip—we won't miss during our staycation. It's also a chance to have a little more fun.

You'll also be further motivated by reading about the rewards of taking a staycation, such as:

- How it can help you connect with your spouse and kids
- How it can create lasting memories, just like a traditional vacation
- How it can give you time to be a tourist in your hometown

Here's another reward:

Knowing that you won't take a flight in which, as the plane reaches cruising altitude, your two-year-old begins projectile vomiting. Can a trip be worse than that?

Actually, yes. There was that Continental Airlines flight in 2007 in which a lavatory overflow sent sewage spilling down the aisle. (Fortunately, the airline did not add a fee for this special in-flight entertainment.)

So those are all rewards of taking a staycation. But you want something more, right? A tangible reward?

Okay, so let's talk about the Staycation Reward. It's what you give yourself at the end of your vacation for saving money on gas, airfare, and a hotel that's overpriced because it's in a tourist area. You can calculate your reward by adding up your savings in fuel, flight, and hotel and cutting that total in half.

That's your reward, which can be used to buy something for yourself or your family. It can be frivolous. It can be pragmatic. It can even be put into an account and applied to your next staycation or traditional vacation.

Or the reward can be used during the staycation to fund a centerpiece element of your time off, such as finishing off a romantic week with a hot air balloon ride.

It's certainly not the kind of spending most people can do each day of a staycation. But one of the staycation rules is to treat yourself, and the Staycation Reward is a way to splurge during your time of financial responsibility.

So for those who want to apply the reward to their staycation, you'll find a Staycation Reward in each chapter. If you're committed to saving the money for practical purposes, that's fine too. But whatever you do, stand by your decision to take a staycation.

Quiz

When you hear that a roller coaster can reach 120 miles per hour, do you ask, "Yeah, but does it also have a double corkscrew or a dive loop?"

Would you like to get the feeling of skydiving without falling thousands of feet in the air?

Have you ever wanted to drive more than 100 miles per hour while knowing that your health and driving record wouldn't be affected?

Does thinking about go-karts, batting cages, video games, and salty popcorn make you feel younger?

Would you like to show your kids that there is no age limit for water slides?

If you answered "yes" to any of the above, you'll find ideas in "Theme Parks and Thrill Rides" to get your staycation speeding down the right track.

Chapter 3
Theme Parks and Thrill Rides

It's the classic vacation for families with kids, but many adults enjoy a trip to a theme park. Places such as Universal Studios, the Sea World parks, and Busch Gardens have thrilling rides, amazing shows, and sodas that still cost more than a gallon of gas.

But the "Big Dogs" of amusement parks, of course, are Disneyland in Anaheim, California, and the Magic Kingdom park of Walt Disney World in Orlando, Florida. They are consistently first and second in the annual worldwide attendance figures, and according to figures from the Themed Entertainment Association and Economics Research Associates, they had a combined attendance of nearly 32 million in 2007.

Those are by far the most popular parks, but you would never know it from the Disney commercials. In the commercials, the parks look nearly abandoned. Adults stroll leisurely on open walkways and kids skip down the street, hand-in-hand with Disney characters, and never smash into a family searching for Tomorrowland. (Or "bathroom land," which is the only land in Disney's kingdom that doesn't include a line.)

YOU CAN TAKE IT WITH YOU

When the sun sets at a theme park, people begin heading to the gift shop with no intention of buying a gift. What these park visitors want, or actually need, is a sweatshirt or jacket to stay warm. Most parks cool down quickly at night and a daytime sunburn leads to evening chills, which then leads to buying overpriced clothing to stay warm during the final hours of a fun day. So remember to pack a jacket or sweatshirt when you head to a theme park, and if you bring along kids, consider buying them a new jacket or sweatshirt that you can show them for the first time at the park. That makes the trip a little more fun. And if you don't want to carry the extra clothes around all day, rent a locker at the park.

Something else you'll never see is footage of one of Disneyland's truly awesome moments: the melee after the park opens in the morning.

It's like the start of a marathon. Screams of "This way, not that way!" and "Hurry, hurry, the lines are getting longer!" fill the air as Disney guests hold their cameras tightly, zip up their fannypacks, and pick up the pace. Strollers reach record speeds and bang into each other like NASCAR drivers edging for position. It's a hectic start to the day, but hey, the ride lines could be expanding like a flesh-eating virus.

Of course they are. It's Disneyland. But we all know that waiting is part of the Disney experience. It's the price you pay—along with admission, parking, stroller rental, and the emotional cost of having your child request a bathroom trip while standing in a long line—to experience Disney excitement.

Okay, enough swipes at the Disney parks. I went to Disneyland a half-dozen times as a kid, and I still find it charming. It's a great destination, but the top draws of all megasized theme parks are the rides, and there are easy ways to bring those kinds of thrills to your staycation.

First, the thinking-inside-the-box answer.

Local and Regional Amusement Parks

Smaller amusement parks, often with rides that are more dizzying than at the biggest parks, are all over the country. Six Flags (*www .sixflags.com*) operates more than a dozen parks in ten states, and each park has amazing rides. One such ride is the Kingda Ka, which

Six Flags says propels you "horizontally at 128 mph via hydraulic launch." In other words, the perfect ride for right after lunch.

Another park operator, Cedar Fair Entertainment (*www.cedarfair.com*), has more than a dozen destinations. That includes Cedar Point in Sandusky, Ohio, which has seventeen roller coasters, more than any other park in the world. One of the coasters, called "Raptor," is an inverted coaster that has seats like a ski lift suspended beneath a track. Riders can look down and see their feet dangling as they go through a vertical loop, two inverted corkscrews, a zero-gravity roll and a "cobra roll" that turns riders upside down twice.

That gives you an idea of the kind of rides available at regional parks. Staycationer Amy D. likes to take her family to Kings Island amusement park near her home in Ohio.

"We did Disney World so we could check it off," Amy said. "It was incredibly expensive and a day at Kings Island is just as good."

Not everyone will agree, but you have lots of amusement parks to choose from. More than 200 U.S. parks are out there to satisfy thrill-seekers (find links to them at *www.themeparkinsider.com*). Many of the parks also offer a second day of admission for only a few dollars more than the price for one day. A two-day pass allows you to move at a more leisurely pace through the park, and perhaps recover from hydraulic launches and cobra rolls.

Skydiving

Now let's think more out of the box . . . and out of the airplane. That's right, skydiving!

Okay, so skydiving might not be your thing. But for many people, it proves to be the ultimate thrill ride. A first-time jump, including instruction, will probably cost at least $200. It's a fun staycation splurge for a thrill-seeker, and you can find a skydiving center near you through the U.S. Parachute Association's website, *www.uspa .org*. Some skydiving schools allow sixteen-year-olds to jump with parental consent, but most require participants to be eighteen.

But what if you want your kids to be involved? Or what if people couldn't pay you to jump out of a plane? Well, you can create the skydive feeling without the fear of a Wile E. Coyote–type splat.

Vertical Wind Tunnels

A vertical wind tunnel is a wind tunnel that moves air up in a vertical column and is sometimes referred to as "indoor skydiving." You fly a few feet off the ground in a stream of air with a net below you, sometimes indoors, sometimes outdoors. Skydivers often use the tunnels for training, but the tunnels are also open for the average Joe or Joan. And although most skydiving companies won't allow kids under age sixteen to jump, kids as young as three can jump into the wind-tunnel experience.

There are more than a dozen of these wind tunnels in the United States and more are in the works as they gain popularity. You can find links and more information for them at *www.body flight.net*, and it's less expensive than you might expect. A two- or three-minute ride, giving you the chance to float like you drank the bubble soda in *Willy Wonka and the Chocolate Factory*, is generally less than $50.

The speed of the wind can be adjusted for anyone from a beginner to a body-flight expert training for skydiving and instructional classes are also available. The tunnels don't take up much room, and it's probably only a matter of time before they begin appearing at amusement parks.

Professional Driving Lessons

Staycations eliminate the long road trip, but they can encourage the road thrill. Racetracks across the country give professional driving lessons and then let the amateur drivers take off around the track like NASCAR stars. Or at least like heavy-footed NASCAR wannabes looking to let it rip after driving a minivan to the track.

I did a story for the *Dallas Morning News* a few years ago about a teenager named Brian who got to take the driving lessons through the Make-A-Wish Foundation, which grants the wishes of kids with life-threatening illnesses. I watched as Brian tore around the track at Texas Motor Speedway in a sports car worth nearly $100,000. (Somewhere, an insurance agent had to be cringing.)

Brian said it was one of the most exhilarating things he had ever done, and you know, teenagers are hard to impress. Brian also offered to drive me around with him, but the driving school wouldn't allow it. Thank goodness.

The driving lessons can cost $250 to $500 at different tracks around the country. That's a little pricey for many staycationers, but it might be worth it as a big highlight of a staycation. You can find links to racetracks that have racing schools at *www.racing schools.com*.

If you're not interested in the lessons, or you don't trust yourself with that much horsepower, you can just purchase a ride with a driving pro. The experience is as impressive as any theme-park thrill ride.

Water Parks

Twenty-five years ago, a metro area might have had only one or two monstrous water parks, which catered mostly to young adults and teenagers seeking big slides and a place to show off their Wayfarer sunglasses.

Many of those huge parks are still around, but smaller ones have sprung up, and now some city pools and recreation centers are built with slides and water playgrounds. All the water parks cater to families, with attractions ranging from leisurely "lazy rivers" and splash areas for toddlers to wild rides such as Dragon's Revenge at Schlitterbahn Water Park Resort in New Braunfels, Texas. That ride includes blasts of water that send a rider uphill and has, in the park's words, "six dark creepy caverns filled with magical special effects including spinning tunnels, theatrical

HOME IS WHERE THE COOL IS

If you haven't been on a water slide in a few years, you should give it a try. Chances are it's more thrilling than dropping a swimsuit size. Water parks are a great low-cost, high-excitement destination for people of all ages. Make it special by finding a hotel near the water park, checking in for a couple of nights, and having food delivered to the hotel room. The bang for the buck will be immense if you have young kids, who will remember the experience long after your next big vacation. And for families with teenagers, getting one hotel room for the parents and another for the kids can be a worthy upgrade.

lighting, fiber optics, riveting original music, aromatic atmosphere, fog, faux fire and an encounter with the angry dragon." If you want to splurge a little, at least for a night or two, try to find a Great Wolf Lodge near you. Each Great Wolf Lodge resort—there are ten in the United States and one in Canada—includes a large indoor water park (find locations at *www.greatwolflodge.com*). There are nearly a dozen other hotels that also have indoor water parks, and you can find them by typing "hotel with indoor water park" into a search engine.

To find a water park near you, visit *www.thewaterparkreview .com*, which has links to water parks across the country. It also has reviews of the parks by people who have visited them.

BMX Racing Tracks

There are hundreds of BMX racing tracks across the country, but wait a second. Can a kid, or a forty-year-old man, just show up at one of the BMX tracks and be part of a race?

In some cases, yes. But I wouldn't recommend it. You could end up wiping out in front of a group of teenagers creating a video for YouTube. It's better to just practice riding around the track, which you can do by paying an hourly or daily admission fee. During a practice run, nobody will be trying to knock you down, you can set your own pace and be as "extreme" as you want to be, and you won't end up on YouTube in a video titled "Check out this dude's crash!"

If riding a BMX bike doesn't sound appealing, you can just watch your kids ride around the track. But being a little adventurous is a great way to make a staycation day stand out from the everyday. You can find a list of tracks at *www.ababmx.com*, which is the homepage of the American Bicycle Association.

Zipping down a BMX track might not be right for everyone, but it's fun and inexpensive. You can also ask the tracks about renting a bike and helmet. Skateboard parks are another idea, although better for kids. The only reason to take up skateboarding as an adult is to test the limits of your health insurance.

Family Fun Centers

Twenty-five years ago, most family fun centers were places for miniature golf, video games, and not much more. But that was back when arcades were filled with games like Centipede and Donkey Kong and the snack bar didn't go beyond Slushees, hot dogs, and popcorn so salty that you needed to buy a second Slushee. It was a great business model.

But what do you get at today's family fun centers?

Well, probably not Centipede and Donkey Kong, unless they are stashed in a corner dedicated to video antiques. Today's video games are about 3-D, virtual reality, and graphics that make Super Mario Brothers look like Pong from the early seventies. But as amazing as today's arcade games have become, they are only a small part of family fun centers. Many of the centers have evolved into small-scale amusement parks with bowling, go-kart tracks for adults and kids, bumper boats, batting cages, roller coasters, and laser tag arenas where adults can be humiliated by ten-year-olds. Some family fun centers even have fields for paintball.

Spending three or four hours, or even a whole day, at a fun center is easy. Before you go, call the front desk and ask if they have

Staycation Reward: Theme Parks and Thrill Rides

Many theme parks now offer passes that eliminate the biggest downside of their big rides: the long, long, long wait in line. Some passes will electronically stand in line for you and then alert you when it's your turn to ride. Others actually allow you to cut in front of people and trim your wait time about 75 percent. It's a great idea for anyone who has stood in a two-hour line for a two-minute ride thinking, "This better be one heck of a ride." (Or for parents who have stood in a line of any length for a ride in a ladybug car that goes about five miles per hour.)

Of course, the convenience comes at a price. A pass will probably more than double the cost of admission. That makes it tougher on a budget, but if a day at an amusement park is a highlight of your staycation, it's a place to splurge. You can stay out of the heat longer, and you might get on twice as many rides.

You could also consider buying season passes for theme parks and water parks. They are a big expense up front, but can easily pay for themselves if you use them enough. Also consider memberships at indoor climbing facilities or taking part in a rock-climbing trip. If you or someone in your family is big into BMX racing, you could save money on gear rental by buying the equipment. Again, this is a big cost upfront, but can really make sense in the long run if you use the equipment enough.

any "all you can play" specials that allow you to pay a set fee for unlimited attractions. You can find a list of fun centers at *www .funcenterdirectory.com*. For entertainment centers that are better for older kids and adults, try Dave and Buster's (*www.daveandbusters .com*) or GameWorks (*www.gameworks.com*). They have a combined sixty-five locations in the United States.

Many of the entertainment centers, whether for families or adults, have restaurants with menus that go beyond hot dogs and pizza. But you'll still find the Slushees. The popcorn is still available, too, and as salty as ever. But that's okay. Have another Slushee. You're on vacation.

Rock Climbing

The "It's totally extreme!" craze continues in the United States, but I'm guessing most staycationers won't be interested in finding a place to street luge, bungee jump, or leap off a roof into a pool. But although rock climbing is often grouped with extreme sports, it's really a mainstream activity. It's safe, too, unless you want to try free solo climbing, which involves no ropes, harnesses, or protective gear.

That's a little too thrilling for most of us. But indoor rock climbing will do nicely, and you'll find a list of climbing facilities at *www .indoorclimbing.com*. Climbing is available at climbing gyms and fitness clubs across the country, and even if you've never climbed before, there are instructional classes and beginner level climbing paths. For outdoor climbing, you can check into day trips in your area. Local climbing groups are easy to find by calling a climbing gym near you or searching the Internet for your city and "climbing day trips."

Ready, Set, Stay

Disneyland and Disney World are expensive, crowded, and at times, annoying. But to say any other amusement park can replace it is ridiculous. Toni S., a frequent staycationer who has also traveled to both Disney parks, describes it this way:

"If you want to escape to a totally different environment which is both entertaining and offers some thrills, I would definitely go with Disney."

So would I. But with a staycation, we focus on the positive. And the positive side is that you can include amusement park thrills in your staycation even if an amusement park isn't nearby. You can also make sure that a trip to a smaller amusement park, water park, or any kind of park is more than run of the mill.

Stay at a hotel right by the amusement park so you can get up early and be one of the first in line. Try rides that you never dared try before. If you would do it on a "real" vacation, do it on a staycation.

Take lots of pictures, too, and buy souvenirs. With the money you've saved on your staycation, you can afford at least one goofy thing from the gift shop. And if you need something Goofy, or Mickey or Minnie, head to a Disney store or check out *www .disneystore.com*.

Help on the Net

- *www.themeparkinsider.com*: List and links to more than 200 U.S. theme parks, plus reviews and advice

- *www.sixflags.com*: Six Flags, Inc. operates twenty-one theme parks and water parks in the United States and Canada
- *www.cedarfair.com*: Cedar Fair Entertainment Co. operates seventeen theme and water parks in the United States and Canada
- *www.rcdb.com*: Rollercoaster database searchable by location, name, and design (bobsled, standup, suspended, etc.)
- *www.thrillnetwork.com*: News, reviews, and forums about theme parks
- *www.themeparks.about.com/cs/waterparks*: List of water parks by state, plus a slide guide
- *www.thewaterparkreview.com*: Water park reviews categorized by state
- *www.racingschools.com*: Links to nationwide racetracks that have racing schools
- *www.uspa.org*: U.S. Parachute Association's list of skydiving schools throughout country
- *www.bodyflight.net*: Links to vertical wind tunnels in the United States
- *www.bungeezone.com*: Links to companies that offer bungee jumping, categorized by state
- *www.ababmx.com*: American Bicycle Association's links to BMX tracks in the United States
- *www.funcenterdirectory.com*: Links to family fun centers across the country
- *www.daveandbusters.com, www.gameworks.com*: Entertainment centers with restaurants and games for adults and older kids
- *www.indoorclimbing.com*: List of climbing facilities in the United States

Quiz

Would you like to enjoy a scenic mountain view without having to climb a mountain?

Is watching a marshmallow roast over a campfire one of your great childhood memories?

Would you like a way to show your kids that blueberries and strawberries aren't grown in plastic containers?

Does floating down a river on a tube, raft, or boat—while listening to music and holding a cold drink—sound like a good way to relax?

Would you like to hike or bike along a trail that includes seeing wildlife and a chance to have a picnic while watching the sun set?

If you answered "yes" to any of the above, you'll find ideas in "Outdoors and Adventure" to get your staycation back to nature.

Chapter 4
Outdoors and Adventure

When I was in the third or fourth grade, my mom bought camping gear for the entire family and reserved a campground spot for Father's Day weekend. It was a surprise for my dad, and there's no doubt he was surprised.

After all, he wasn't the outdoorsy type. He had never expressed any interest in pitching a tent and roughing it. Not by himself, not with my mom, and certainly not with three kids and a dog that would ignore the call of the wild for a Milk Bone and a spot on the couch.

But then we got to the campsite. The fresh mountain air, the beautiful scenery, the peace and quiet . . . that was great for a Father's Day getaway. My dad was able to sit back in a lawn chair, enjoy the great outdoors, and experience how relaxing getting back to nature can be.

For about five minutes, anyway. He spent the rest of the weekend cursing the tent stakes that wouldn't stay in place, worrying about his kids falling off a cliff, and telling us to stop throwing pinecones at each other. It just wasn't his thing.

However, many people enjoy the great outdoors and there is something very special about sitting around a crackling campfire with your family and friends. There's also few better

YOU CAN TAKE IT WITH YOU

Some people call duct tape the "ultimate material" because it can be used for a quick fix when you don't have the time—or know-how—to repair something properly. That makes it an essential part of camping gear, regardless of whether you're sleeping under the stars, in a tent, or in a cabin. Duct tape can be used to repair tears in a sleeping bag, tent, backpack, raincoat, and tarp, and it can even hold together a splintering tent pole or the broken leg of a chair. Unfortunately, even the ultimate material doesn't work on sunburns, poison ivy, or bug bites, so remember the calamine lotion. If you don't have room in your bag for it, duct tape it to the inside of your car.

ways to bond with your kids than to get them away from their electronic addictions for a couple of days. Actually, the same bonding experience can happen for couples who spend their daily lives stuck in the techno-web.

Camping close to home is easy, too. Campgrounds are available at state parks, national parks, and other public recreation areas. They're dirt cheap, and many have onsite showers and bathrooms so you can determine your level of wilderness immersion. You really don't need any camping knowledge, either. If you want to catch and prepare fish for dinner, great. If you want to swing by KFC for a bucket of chicken to pass around the campfire, there's nothing wrong with that. Camping can be whatever you want it to be.

There are, however, some good rules to follow. They can be summed up in one sentence: Leave no trace.

When camping, it's good to follow the seven principles set forth by the Leave No Trace Center for Outdoor Ethics, a nonprofit organization dedicated to promoting the responsible use of the outdoors.

The principles are:

- Plan ahead and prepare
- Travel and camp on durable surfaces (established trails and campsites)
- Dispose of waste properly
- Leave what you find
- Minimize campfire impacts
- Respect wildlife
- Be considerate of other visitors

You can find out more at *www.lnt.org*.

Camping and Hiking

Spending a vacation outdoors immediately brings camping to mind. But even if camping isn't high on your list of interests, you can still give your staycation an outdoorsy element. It can be as simple as taking a day hike. Do that and you'll find beautiful views such as the scenic dam overlook at Lake Poway in Poway, California, the scenic waterfalls at Grayson Highlands State Park in Virginia, or the sandstone rock formations in Woodland Park, Colorado.

Chances are good that you're more than 100 miles from those hikes. But the chances are excellent that there are parks, trails, and sightseeing spots in your hometown or nearby. You can find regional hiking guides such as *www.localhikes.com* on the Internet. It's good to research a hike first to make sure it's not too strenuous for you and your hiking group. You can also find trails for hiking and mountain biking at *www.americantrails.org*, which has a database of nearly 1,000 trails that are on federal, state, city, and private lands and are designated as National Recreation Trails. Each trail synopsis will let you know what to expect on the trail, including scenery and difficulty.

If you want to give your hiking or biking trip more of a vacation feel, end it with a massage treatment or other pampering (see "The Pampered Life" chapter for more on that). Make it even better by adding in dinner at a restaurant you've never tried and a night at a local hotel.

Some more outdoors-related ideas are below. If the weather is nice during your planned staycation, getting away from the city, even just forty or fifty miles away, is an easy way to make your staycation feel far from your daily routine. And for those of you who, like me, aren't the outdoorsy type, remember that a staycation is a great opportunity to try something new. Maybe you'll even see me, a Boy Scout dropout, trying to put up a tent and telling my kids to stop throwing pinecones at each other.

Rafting Trips, "River Floats," and Tubing

Before my wife and I had kids, we visited Royal Gorge Park in Cañon, Colorado, a beautiful area near Colorado Springs. Janell and I walked over the Royal Gorge Bridge, which at more than 1,000 feet off the ground is the world's highest suspension bridge. The bridge will support in excess of two million pounds, we were told, but feeling it move slightly as cars passed over it was pretty wild.

We also traveled on the Royal Gorge Scenic Railway. The view was fantastic, but what I remember the most were the people shooting the rapids in the Arkansas River next to the railway. Now *that* looked wild, and in some cases, just plain

STAYCATION BONUS #2: AVOIDING SECURITY CHECKPOINTS
First you take off your shoes and send them through the X-ray machine with your carry-on bag, jacket, laptop computer, keys, mobile phone, and a small baggy filled with liquids under three ounces. After collecting everything, and making sure you still have your ID and ticket, you walk to the checkpoint's designated area for putting shoes back on. That's where a dozen travelers in socks are headed and about three chairs are available. The travelers who don't find a chair hobble around, trying to put on their shoes while hoping nobody is videotaping their awkward moves. So here's your second staycation bonus: There's no security checkpoint in your own car.

scary. I kept waiting for the kayaker to get stuck on a group of rocks, probably because I've seen too many episodes of *America's Funniest Home Videos*.

Man-versus-whitewater might be a little too thrilling for most people, but rafting trips, river floats, and tubing are for everyone. Much milder, but still a lot of fun. Sometimes the river trips are on public land and organized by city recreation departments, while others are privately operated.

Rivers and lakes for tubing and rafting often have campsites as well, creating an easy two- or three-day getaway. Some trips also include concerts, cookouts, and fireside singing.

Another way to have fun on the water is by heading to a lake and renting personal watercraft such as a WaveRunner, Jet Ski, or Sea-Doo. Pontoon boats are also available, and are great for families or a couple of families who can split the cost. Speedboat rentals and tours can also add excitement to a trip to the lake.

Off-Roading Rentals and Excursions

Many states have businesses that offer scenic off-road tours. In Arizona, a four-hour Jeep excursion includes a tour of desert scenery and a chance to pan for gold. The tour also includes potato-gun shooting and a chance to feed coyotes. Real coyotes, not the pro hockey team in Phoenix, although that also would be pretty cool.

That's an example of the off-roading tours available throughout the country. The prices can be up to $100 a person, but that's for nearly a full day of fun. There are sunset tours with dinner included, tours of the wine country, mountain tours, and tours specific to every region of the country. A good way to locate one is by typing "Jeep tour" and your state into an Internet search engine.

Jeep rentals are also available if you want to take the wheel. Renting a four-door will allow you to take five adults on the trip. If you already have an off-road vehicle and would like to find a place to explore, you can find an off-roading club near you at *www .offroaders.com.*

Ski Lifts in Offseason

Are you a skier?

If so, you know how packed and expensive ski resorts are in the winter. But when the snow melts, many ski areas keep their lifts in service for incredible and inexpensive sightseeing opportunities. It's a great idea for families or romantic outings, and you might be surprised to find how many ski facilities there are in the United States. At *www.goski.com*, you'll find ski resorts in thirty-seven states.

You can probably get an all-day lift ticket for about $15. Some resorts offer hiking areas at the top of the lifts and have picnic spots. Others, such as Vail Resort in Colorado and Stowe Mountain in Vermont, offer twilight gondola rides to watch the sunset.

These rides have become popular enough at resorts that ride-and-lunch packages are often available.

Aside from the lifts and gondola rides, ski resorts have a variety of attractions during the summer, including nature hikes and mountain biking lessons and rides. No fresh powder, but perhaps a refreshing day for your staycation.

Free Wildlife Viewing Areas

Even if you're gridlocked in the big city, you're not far from seeing wildlife more exotic than stray cats and unfortunate animals that didn't make it across the street.

Imagine seeing animals such as bighorn sheep at the Fort Robinson State Park in Nebraska, a wild boar at the Nantahala River wetlands in North Carolina, or a mountain goat at Timberwolf Mountain in Washington. If you live in New Mexico, you can visit Cienega Canyon and see Abert squirrels and a broad-tailed hummingbird. Your kids will be able to tell their friends that they saw a red-naped sapsucker, and when those friends ask if "red-naped sapsucker" can really rock, they'll be able to say, "red-naped sapsucker isn't a band; it's a bird."

So how do you find the free wildlife viewing spot near you? Just check the complete list at *www.wildlifeviewingareas.com*. The website allows you to search by area or for a type of animal you're looking for. Information for each wildlife viewing area also includes the animals you will find there.

At many of the viewing spots, guides are available to help spot wildlife. Probably even some savvy Boy Scouts who, unlike

HOME IS WHERE THE TENT IS

Camping isn't for everyone. But you can cheat with a backyard campout. Without giving up the secure feeling of having your house nearby, you can have the s'mores, the flashlight games, the search for constellations, the ghost stories, and the shadow puppets on the tent. Bringing the camp to you is a great way to try camping for the first time. If you're not into sleeping outside with the bugs, you can even camp in your home. Just use some bed sheets to make a tent in the living room and roll out the sleeping bags. It might be goofy, but it will be memorable.

me, didn't add "quitter" to the Scout Law. Camping opportunities are also available, so bring the ingredients for s'mores. Or the bucket of Kentucky Fried Chicken and two liters of soda. You can still call yourself "outdoorsy."

Whale Watching

Whale watching is a fun family activity even if the whale isn't named Shamu. Excursions to see whales, dolphins, and other sea creatures have become popular recreation activities, and they're available on the East and West coasts.

One such excursion, from the San Francisco Bay to the Farallon Islands twenty-seven miles off the California coast, includes the chance to see whales, dolphins, sea birds, sea turtles, and seals. A tour guide will point out the sights and educate visitors about the history of the area.

Staycation Reward: Outdoors and Adventure

I mentioned earlier that my family spent several vacations in San Diego in a rented RV. Those vacations were the most fun I've had with my family. Renting an RV can be expensive, and so is the gas that it will guzzle, but if the rental is limited to a few days and the road trip isn't far, the cost might not be so scary. RV parks offer electric hookups, bathrooms, and shower facilities, and some offer family activities and attractions.

Most whale-watching tours will offer a fun and interesting trip even if you don't see a humpback whale lunging out of the water. A couple of websites, *www.whalewatching.com* and *www.whaleguide .com*, have links to whale-watching excursions. One note of warning before you go: It can be a bumpy ride out on the ocean as you look for whales, so if that might make you queasy, take a pill for motion sickness beforehand.

Horseback Riding

For many people today, the closest they get to horseback riding involves a horse forced to walk in a circle next to a clown making balloon animals. Some kids are lucky enough to learn how to ride horseback at summer camp.

But fortunately, you don't have to own a horse or go to summer camp to do some riding. Search *www.horseandtravel.com* and you'll find riding stables in every state that offer the chance to ride and take lessons in riding. Plan ahead and you can make it part of a camping trip.

Picking Your Own Fruit

This may sound like work, but it's actually fun. The website *www .pickyourown.org* has links to farms across the country that allow visitors to pick their own blueberries, strawberries, apples, peaches, and more, depending on the time of the season. After you finish, you're welcome to take the fruits of your labor home.

Wear some old clothes, bring containers to collect the fruit, and prepare to get dirty. You'll be able to get fruit for cheaper than at the grocery store, but don't do this to save money. Do it as a way to get back to nature. Pack a picnic, find a shady spot, and take your time. If you have kids, some larger farms offer hay rides, corn mazes, and petting zoos.

The Pick Your Own site also has a list of festivals dedicated to a particular food—apple, tomato, corn, peach, and so on—that you can search through. The festivals are usually free and feature foods to sample, baking contests, music, and parades. A lot of pie-eating contests, too, for anyone with a sweet tooth, a competitive streak, and a willingness to be photographed with a face covered with pie.

For those planning a staycation in the fall, consider visiting a farm's pumpkin patch. I enjoy doing that each year at the pumpkin patches near my home. It's also a highlight for my kids, and watching them try over and over to pick up a heavy pumpkin is hilarious (until they drop one on my foot).

If your family is the outdoorsy type, you should consider purchasing a tent and new camping equipment. In many cases, you can buy these items used on websites such as *www.ebay.com* or *www.craigslist.com*. If your family plans on camping often, these items will pay for themselves over time. Consider doing the same with fishing or hiking gear or bicycles.

Ready, Set, Stay

At this point, I've established that I'm not the outdoorsy type. I've also given my parents virtually no credit for taking their kids on any vacations. So to be fair, I'll point out the camping trips we took during the summers of my high school years.

It wasn't exactly camping. My parents rented a motor home for a week or two and we drove from Phoenix to a place called Campland on the Bay in San Diego, where you could hook up your RV to electricity and there were bathrooms, showers, a pool, and the beach nearby.

We slept in the motor home at night, so it wasn't camping. But it had many of the elements: getting away from the everyday routine; the campfires and s'mores; the deep, dark, starry nights; and of course, Sea World. Wait, scratch that last one. But most of all, the Campland vacation meant spending time together as a family.

You get lots of that with camping, whether it's ten miles from home, in another state, or in a tent, cabin, or motor home. It's a great way to create a vacation feel and add some mental distance from your everyday lifestyle.

Help on the Net

- *www.dayhiker.com*: Day hiker resources
- *www.localhikes.com*: Links to local hiking trails nationwide
- *www.gorp.com*: Hiking guides, lists of trails, state-by-state list of rafting rivers
- *www.americantrails.org*: Database of National Recreation Trails
- *www.offroaders.com:* Links to off-roading clubs across the country
- *www.nps.gov:* National Park Service
- *www.goski.com*: Links to ski resorts across the country
- *www.wildlifeviewingareas.com*: List of wildlife viewing areas in the United States
- *www.whalewatching.com, www.whaleguide.com*: Links to whale-watching tours
- *www.horseandtravel.com*: Contact information for riding stables across the country
- *www.pickyourown.org*: List and description of farms that allow visitors to pick fruit
- *www.lovetheoutdoors.com*: Camping tips, links to private and public campsites

Quiz

Does watching an auto assembly line at work, touring an ice cream factory, checking out an offbeat museum, or visiting a brewery that gives out free samples sound interesting?

Would you like to view the rings of Saturn and see a laser show featuring Pink Floyd's *Dark Side of the Moon* on the same night?

Would you like to learn a foreign language, how to make jewelry, and ways to invest the money you save by taking a staycation?

Is part of the reason for your staycation a desire to be more environmentally friendly?

Would you like to know the best ways to maximize trips to zoos, aquariums, museums, and how to use the library to discover books, movies, music, and your ancestors?

If you answered "yes" to any of the above, you'll find ideas in "Educational Staycations" to make sure your time off gets a passing grade.

Chapter 5
Educational Staycations

Okay, here's another rule. I know, I know. You've had it with the rules. But I've got three kids, so I'm very much about rules.

So here's another one:

Never tell your kids that something is educational.

You've probably heard that from other parents or learned it from your kids, so this just serves as a reminder. When your kids are learning about potential and kinetic energy while rolling balls down ramps at the science museum, just let them think it's pure fun. Don't speak a word about learning as they check out the dinosaur exhibits at the nature museum. Just let them absorb the information the way they absorb the unfortunate word you uttered when that van backed into you in the parking lot.

Actually, we don't even have to think about the staycation ideas in this chapter as educational. Sure, zoos, aquariums, and museums, in addition to being hassle-free and inexpensive, are great ways to learn. But they're also fun. It's not like back in high school when you struggled to pay attention in history class.

That kind of struggle won't happen with your staycation. Educational doesn't have to mean lectures, quizzes, and trying to stay awake with one eye closed. It can be a trip to an aviation museum, a historic house tour, or going behind the scenes at a local television station. You can even get an education in rock music by visiting a planetarium to see a laser light show tribute to the Red Hot Chili Peppers. (Unlike the band, however, you'll have to stay fully clothed during the performance.)

Factory Tours and Company Museums

The idea of a factory tour might make you mutter "third-grade field trip." There's good reason for that. The tour of the dairy production plant is as much a part of the elementary-school experience as crayons, superhero lunch boxes, and covering your hands with glue and then pretending to peel it off like skin.

But let's forget about the kids for a while. Factory tours are great for adults, and they're all over the country. Just north of Seattle, for example, you can see airplanes in various stages of assembly at a Boeing plant. In Dearborn, Michigan, you can see an automobile assembly line at work at the Ford Rouge Factory Tour. In Memphis, you can tour the Gibson guitar factory and watch the process of creating a guitar.

Company museums are also great. In Milwaukee, there's the Harley-Davidson Museum, where you can view exhibits celebrating the products, history, and culture of the motorcycle company. In Atlanta, there's the World of Coca-Cola, which has the world's largest collection of Coke memorabilia and a functioning bottling line that produces eight-ounce bottles of Coke. It's part museum and part amusement center, because it also has a 3-D movie theater with moving seats. (I'm not sure what the movie is about. Maybe a Coke bottle chases a Pepsi bottle.)

One of the best tours I've taken was at the Coors Brewery in Golden, Colorado. Coors has now merged with Miller, but the tour at the brewery is still available. You don't have to be a big beer drinker to enjoy seeing memorabilia and touring the production plant. Also, it's a free tour, and you get to sample lots of beer at the end of the tour. Not little medicine cups of beer—really good-sized

HOW IT'S MADE

If you like the way factory tours give you a behind-the-scenes look, you'll enjoy the television show *How It's Made*. The show, which airs on the Science Channel, shows how everyday products such as bubblegum, guitars, contact lenses, manhole covers, and engines are made. It's a great show for kids, so if you're looking for something to keep them busy for a couple of hours between activities, record a few episodes and let them watch something entertaining and educational.

glasses. No charge. If you're not near one of the large breweries, check for a smaller brewery in your area. Many of them offer tours as well, such as the brewery that Katie and Chris visited during their staycation in northern California.

Katie and Chris, who had planned to visit New York City before the price of flying spiked, toured a sake brewery. For those who don't know, sake (pronounced "sa-key") is a Japanese alcoholic beverage made from rice.

"They have beautifully landscaped grounds and a good self-guided tour," Katie said. "Plus a sake-tasting at the end!"

But Why So Cheap?

So why do so many companies offer tours for free or at wallet-friendly prices?

It's simple, really. It makes business sense. Tours are great for a company's public image. That's why the companies will treat you so well, and that's why factory tours and company museums are a perfect idea for a staycation. It's a win-win for company and staycationer.

You won't need to travel far to find a good tour. The site *www.factorytoursusa.com* has links to more than 500 of them. You'll find the Trek bicycle company in Whitewater, Wisconsin; the American Whistle Corp. in Columbus, Ohio; and the Louisville Slugger Museum in, you guessed it, Louisville, Kentucky. And remember the staycation rule that discussed buying souvenirs? At the Louisville Slugger Museum, you can get your name engraved on a bat. As souvenirs go, that's a grand slam.

It's also easy to find tours for kids, such as at the Ben & Jerry's factory in Waterbury, Vermont; the Jelly Belly factory in Fairfield, California; and the Crayola factory in Easton, Pennsylvania. And one you probably haven't heard of is the Carousel Magic Carousel Factory in Mansfield, Ohio. There you can watch workers carving the wooden horses for carousels across the country.

Tours can be found throughout the country, and they are a fun way to spend a few hours, which is why Melissa M. makes them a part of her staycations in Massachusetts.

"The two dollars we spend on a factory tour puts us in touch with local producers of nationally recognized products like Vermont Teddy Bears, Ben & Jerry's ice cream, Cabot cheese, Magic Hat Brewery, and on and on," she said. "The list within three hours of where we live is nearly endless."

You'll probably find lots to choose from near your home, too. But if none of the more than 500 factory tours listed are within driving distance, you can still find a tour for your staycation. Most newspapers give tours of their facilities, including their printing facilities. Television and radio stations will also let you tour facilities if you call ahead of time. Again, we're talking about companies eager to reach out to the community, make a good impression, and find new readers, viewers, and listeners. Even if they don't have formal tours, they'll be very accommodating.

Fire and Police Stations

For those of you with kids, here's one final idea for a tour: the local fire station. Many fire departments offer formal tours of their stations and most others will take the time to show you around if you call in advance.

This is a big hit with my kids. My boys went to a birthday party at a fire station, which included a tour of the station, climbing on a fire truck, and seeing all the protective clothing and equipment a firefighter uses.

It's great to feed the curiosity of kids, so whatever they're interested in, look into a tour. You won't find formal tours of the pinsetters at a bowling alley or the projection room at a theater, but if you ask politely, the businesses might open some "employees only" doors for you.

Staycationers Brenda and Ed have a great example of that. They have a four-year-old son who, like nearly every four-year-old boy, wants to be a firefighter. He likes the heroism, the fire trucks, and the uniform, Brenda said, but mostly he likes the siren. Here's how Brenda tells it:

"We were low on funds and decided we'd just stay close to home and take day trips. We live in a small city, so we phoned our local fire station to see if they gave tours and they said 'Not really,' but stop on by and they'd show us around.

"They took us through the fire station with emphasis on the break room, but the big event was getting to look at and inside the fire truck. The fireman put an official fireman hat on my son, which swallowed most of his face. He was thrilled. But the big surprise was the realization that we were just as excited as he was. Ed and I felt like two big kids."

Those firefighters really are great, even when they're not fighting fires.

Special Museum Programs

You can probably spend an entire staycation at museums. And they can be even better if you look into the special programs offered and their special events calendars online. Science and nature museums often have classes in gardening or "green" living, and art museums have wine-tasting nights that include food and live music. At the Heard Museum in Phoenix, Arizona, the annual Spanish Market includes furniture, jewelry, tilework, paintings, carvings, pottery, and strolling musicians. Most museums also offer lectures that can give you more insight into the exhibits than you would get by walking through the museum on your own.

The important thing, as in the staycation rules, is to plan ahead. If you sign up for e-mail newsletters and alerts from a museum, which you can usually do on its website, you'll know what exhibits, touring shows, and programs are coming up. That will give you an important head start because many popular museum programs have limited space and fill up quickly. That's certainly the case for the new trend of "museum sleepovers," which allows camping inside a museum. Those are especially geared to kids, so I'll talk more about the sleepovers in the "Especially for Kids" chapter.

The "Other" Museums

Museums are educational, but they don't have to fit the traditional educational mold. After hitting the science and natural history museums, try something like the Pez Museum in Burlingame, California, which has every Pez dispenser ever made. Or the International Spy Museum in Washington, D.C., where you can view spy technology of the past, present, and future and test your surveillance skills in interactive exhibits. There's also the Museum of Bad Art in Dedham, Massachusetts, which is truly hilarious, and the Dental Museum in Philadelphia, which will make you feel really good about how far dentistry has come.

And did you know there's also a museum entirely devoted to the king of all canned meats, SPAM? The SPAM Museum is in Austin, Minnesota, but it's the kind of offbeat museum you'll find all over the country. You'll find links to many of them by doing a web search for "unusual museums."

YOU CAN TAKE IT WITH YOU

A way to make a museum visit more fun for kids is to create a scavenger hunt list and bring it along. Before the trip, check the museum's website to learn about some of the attractions your kids will enjoy. At a science and nature museum, for example, kids could search for items such as a picture of a space shuttle, the fossil of a reptile that swam, and an exhibit that uses solar energy. The items can be more specific when you know more about what's in the museum. If you're taking a tour of a company that makes products of special interest to kids, such as the Basic Brown Bear Factory in California or the Hershey's Chocolate World in Pennsylvania, have the kids bring a list of questions they want answered. It gets them more involved.

You don't need to be Clark Griswold in *Vacation*, who led his family to see the second-largest ball of twine on Earth. But if you're bending the definition of a vacation, you can also bend the idea of what a museum has to be. Until writing this book, I didn't know that a Cockroach Hall of Fame existed. It turns out this bizarre, but interesting, museum is in the city where I live.

Observatories and Planetariums

Much like museums, observatories and planetariums offer tours, exhibits, and special programs. Unlike museums, however, there are probably a lot of people who don't know the difference. It's nothing to be ashamed of, unlike the Americans who think that New Mexico is a foreign country and that Condoleezza Rice is a side dish at Chili's.

An observatory is a location equipped with telescopes for observing the planets, stars, and other heavenly bodies (insert your inappropriate "heavenly bodies" remark here). A planetarium is a theater with a large

THE GREEN STAYCATION
A staycation is a great opportunity to take steps toward a more environmentally friendly lifestyle. During your time at home, consider creating a compost bin in your backyard (find out how at *www.howtocompost.org*). Then, take a look around your house and try to pinpoint ways that your family can make your household more energy efficient. If that gets you motivated, try volunteering with a local environmental organization, which can be found through *www.volunteermatch.org*. Your whole staycation doesn't have to be dedicated to Mother Earth, but mix in a few green ideas and you'll know that your staycation is helping the planet.

dome-shaped projection screen that is often used for presenting shows about astronomy. Both are great to visit, and you can find a list of them at *www.astronomyclubs.com*.

Most public observatories allow visitors to look through their huge, powerful telescopes. They also schedule "star parties" that include an observatory staff member explaining what you're looking at through the telescope. Astronomyclubs.com includes links to observatory websites, so you can check out their calendars for special events. Some observatories even offer private star parties in which a staff member will bring a telescope to your backyard and direct your viewing of the sky. Expect to pay some real money for that, however.

Planetariums also have great special programs and shows. Some are for kids, such as "The Sky Above Mr. Rogers's Neighborhood," which has played at many planetariums. For adults, there are laser light shows synchronized to music. Some of the bands featured in these laser shows are Pink Floyd, U2, Dave Matthews Band, Bob Marley, the Beatles, Aerosmith, and the Beastie Boys.

My sixth-grade teacher was right. Science can be fun.

Zoos and Aquariums

In the Outdoors and Adventure chapter, we talked about wildlife viewing areas. The most convenient one, of course, is the zoo. Not quite the same as viewing animals in their natural settings, but still fun and educational.

I learn something new on each trip to the zoo, sometimes from watching the animals, sometimes from reading facts about them, and sometimes from shooting five minutes of video of an elephant. (In that case, I learned that we shoot way too much video.)

What to take video of is your decision, but zoos and aquariums are great staycation destinations. And you can do more than just show up at the zoo like everyone else. Check for special programs like the Bike-About at the San Francisco Zoo, which allows people to bring their bikes to the zoo for a riding tour in the morning before the park opens to the public. Your local zoo might have something like the ZooCool in North Carolina, which is a neat

GETTING THE DISCOUNT

Before you visit any attraction with your kids, get on the Internet and search for the name of the place where you're going, your city, and "coupon and discount." A lot of family attractions now post discounts and coupons on community websites and family message boards. You can even call up the place where you're going and ask if they have any discounted tickets available. It's hard for them to say no to a potential customer.

event during a weekend in August. During the last ZooCool, animals got ice treats to eat and play with as zookeepers explained to visitors how the animals stay cool in the summer. The North Carolina Zoo also had a singer perform and a snow machine that blew snowflakes into the air.

Your local zoo probably has similar programs and events, and it might have a behind-the-scenes tour. These tours, also available at aquariums, allow visitors to meet the animal caretakers, watch feedings, and tour areas inaccessible to the general public. These can be expensive, so consider how interested your family might be before investigating further.

Also, just like the museum trend, zoos are now offering overnight camping on their grounds. That's right, you can climb over the rail and sleep with the monkeys or kangaroos.

Actually, you'll get injured (and probably arrested) if you try to do that. But the zoos do offer overnight camping, and you can read more about it in the "Especially for Kids" chapter.

Getting to Know Your City

If you're like me, there are many things you don't know about the area where you live. What are the stories behind historic sites? Who are the people who helped build the city? How have the neighborhoods changed as the city has grown? A staycation is a great opportunity to learn more. But how do you do that?

"Explore the town through the eyes of a tourist," said Joslyn T., a Dallas-area staycationer.

You can find homes to visit in your area by searching the Internet for your city or state and "historic house." You can also find a list of vintage home museums, categorized by state, at *www.vpa.org*. That's the homepage of the Victorian Preservation Association of Santa Clara Valley, California, but you'll find links to all types of historic homes.

HOME IS WHERE THE HISTORY IS: HISTORIC HOUSE TOURS

An easy way to experience the history of your city is to find a neighborhood with historic homes. The convention and visitors bureau can help you find them, and some older neighborhoods have home tours or restored homes that serve as museums.

Think about what places in your area you would suggest out-of-town guests visit during their stay. There are probably some tourist traps you could do without, but looking at the town through the eyes of a tourist does make a lot of sense. That's why it's good to check out the website of your city's convention and visitors bureau when planning your staycation. Newspaper websites also generally have lists of the top attractions in the area and calendars with upcoming events, and if you're going to be a tourist, you should have a tourist guidebook. It's true even if you're playing tourist in the city where you live. You can find the guidebooks at the bookstore or online at sites such as *www.lonelyplanet.com*, *www.fodors.com*, and the one I find most helpful, *www.frommers.com*.

All the resources above can direct you to city sightseeing tours, historic sites to visit, entertainment districts, nightlife, restaurants, shopping, and other attractions in your city. Some you'll know about, but you'll also find some surprises.

The Wonderful, Underused Library

I remember when I learned how to use the library. My elementary school classmates and I sat cross-legged in front of the librarian, who told us how to take care of books, how we needed to talk softly in the library, and how important it was to learn the Dewey Decimal System and the library's card catalog. If we didn't know how to use the card catalog, how would we ever find a book?

The Internet changed that. But libraries have changed a lot, in other ways, over the years. You can get books there to read during your staycation, of course, but you can also get audio books, CDs, and DVDs; search research databases; and take computer classes.

They have magazines to browse through and newspapers from across the country. There are activities for kids, book discussion groups for adults, and special events for everyone.

A staycation offers the time to relax and explore more of what the library has to offer. Just browsing through a collection of recent magazines is a relaxing way to spend a few hours. And unless you forget to bring back what you borrow, it's all free.

If you have kids, one idea is to use the library to research "theme days" for your staycation. Let the kids pick the subject, such as "ice cream" or "skateboards" or "dinosaurs," and have them find books on the topic. The rest of the day can be dedicated to that subject, with movies, music, food, games, and trips to local attractions. It teaches the kids how much is available at the library, and they'll like having a say in the planning of the staycation.

One last thing to point out about libraries is that they are a great place to find coupons and sometimes even passes. Family attractions such as sporting events, water parks, family amusement centers, children's theaters, and museums often post fliers there with discount offers. Sometimes they can be found on a library bulletin board that is open to public announcements.

Climbing the Family Tree

One way to spend your staycation is to research genealogy. Many people have made interesting discoveries by digging into their family histories, and libraries are a great source for a genealogical project. You will find access to thousands of databases that have records for births, deaths, marriages, adoptions, and beyond.

Staycation Reward: Educational Staycations

I cut short the discussion of zoo VIP tours earlier in the book because they can be expensive. But if you have more than a casual interest in zoos, or your child is really into animals, the special tours might be worth the price. You get to find out animals' names, listen to stories about them, and see how they are fed and cared for.

Aquariums also offer special VIP tours for an added price, so check with your local zoo or aquarium to see what's available. Enrolling in an annual membership might include special privileges like a behind-the-scenes tour, and if you plan on visiting a few times during the year, an annual membership makes sense.

Another idea is buying a family telescope, which can be found for as little as $100. It's a great way to end a staycation that includes a trip to an observatory or planetarium. Science and art day camps, which can be found through local museums, can also be chances to splurge for your kids. If your budget is tighter, maybe just buying an item or two from a museum gift shop will make the trip feel more special. And if your budget isn't as tight, finishing a staycation with a new family computer can be the ultimate educational reward.

But you don't have to find that many branches on your tree to create a fun family research project, especially for kids. Have them call grandparents, aunts, uncles, and other relatives to ask them about their favorite childhood memories. Then they can put together a scrapbook of stories and photos that becomes a great memento. Or the kids can just talk to Mom and Dad about their memories of growing up. Kids love to hear those stories from their parents. Well, at least until the kids are about sixteen years old, and they're tired of hearing the "walked three miles to school in the snow, uphill both ways" story.

School: Not Just for Your Kids

Quiz: If a city recreation department is offering a class for residents, which one do you think it would be?

a. How to Parent a Terrible Two
b. Introduction to Microdermabrasion
c. Basics of Estate Planning

It might surprise you that it could be any one of them. Most cities have recreation departments that organize courses that are for residents and are taught by residents. The variety of courses will depend on the size of your city, but if you search through a city course catalog, in print or online, you'll probably find something that catches your eye. Some of the classes meet once, others several times over a few weeks. They are generally inexpensive.

You'll find classes on topics such as parenting, makeovers, photography, interior decorating, investing, auto repair, jewelry making, sign language, hypnotherapy, and how to make greeting cards. There are also sports classes and workshops that parents and kids can take together. In my city's last catalog, I saw a class called "Fossil Finders" that included a trip to a local creek to look for fossils.

Look into the courses that your own community center or recreation department offers, or try enrolling in a continuing education course at a community college in your area. You'll find classes to advance careers, such as in the business and medical fields. But you'll also find noncredit courses in subjects such as art, music, gardening, financial management, computer training, and physical fitness.

You can even learn how to write poetry to send a romantic letter to your mate while he or she reads the adults-only chapter in this book. No, no . . . don't turn to that chapter yet. It's a surprise. Also, there are no photos, so get your mind out of the gutter.

Ready, Set, Stay

Science and nature museums, history museums, art museums, aviation museums, anthropology museums, children's museums, company museums . . . the list goes on and on. You really can fill an entire staycation soaking up museums.

When you get your fill of museums, consider other educational options like visiting a photo exhibition or taking a beginner's course in a foreign language (Berlitz language schools can be found at *www.berlitz.com*).

The trick is to get your mind thinking creatively, like staycationers Brenda and Ed. One of their favorite staycation activities—and it's educational, too—is to watch meteor showers in their backyard. Every August, the Perseid meteor shower lights up the sky as the Earth crosses the path of Comet Swift-Tuttle. That's the educational part for Brenda and Ed's kids.

The fun part is when the whole family rolls out blankets in the backyard, lies down in a row, and looks up at the sky in the wee hours of the morning. Sometimes they can see fifty or more streaking meteors per hour, and they compete to see who can see the most meteors and find the meteors with the longest streaks.

"We only do this in the backyard now," Brenda said, "because one year we were lined up like this in our driveway and we not only got some very strange stares by neighbors, but someone stopped to ask if we were all right."

They were fine. Great, actually. Creating wonderful memories for their kids and themselves.

Help on the Net

- *www.factorytoursusa.com*: Links to more than 500 factory tours
- *www.museumnetwork.com*: Listings and links to 37,000 museums, searchable by area
- *www.astronomyclubs.com*: Links to observatories and planetariums across the country
- *www.classtrips.com*: Links to destinations and day trips for kids
- *www.howtocompost.org*: Composting how-to for beginners
- *www.berlitz.com*: Links to language training centers and online classes
- *www.volunteermatch.org*: Search your hometown for volunteer opportunities
- *www.genealogylinks.net*: Links to genealogy resources, searchable by state
- *www.aza.org*: Association of Zoos and Aquariums has links to member zoos
- *www.thegreenguide.com*: National Geographic Society's info and ideas about green living
- *www.vpa.org*: List of vintage home tours, categorized by state

Quiz

Do you wonder if it's possible to get a relaxing massage for a price that won't make you tighten up?

Would you consider staying in a hotel in your hometown as a way to break away from your daily routine?

Have you wondered how to find an inexpensive way to get a manicure and pedicure, and have your hair and makeup done?

Would having the time to work with a personal trainer help kickstart your fitness goals?

Would you like to create a spa experience at home with facials, body scrubs, baths, and scalp and hair treatments?

If you answered "yes" to any of the above, you'll find ideas in "The Pampered Life" to make your staycation feel luxurious.

Chapter 6
The Pampered Life

YOU CAN TAKE IT WITH YOU

For the typically tired and hungry traveler, the hotel minibar could be a great customer service. Unfortunately, the prices are so inflated that you wonder if the $8 beer and the $4 bag of pretzels were imported from the moon. So if you're going to make a hotel stay part of your staycation, bring along treats to enjoy in your room and some drinks in a cooler. Many affordable hotels now have in-room mini fridges for guests to use, so check with a hotel before booking your room. It's a nice convenience, and a cold beer or soda tastes better when it doesn't cost more than a gallon of gas.

People have different opinions on what it means to be pampered. For some, it's lying on a deck chair by a pool. For others, it may mean having someone do the cooking and cleaning for them. For many, it means massages and spa treatments.

That leads us to the ultimate pampered vacation: the stay at the upscale resort. Relaxing, luxurious, exciting, and, of course, expensive. Even without a stay at the resort, however, you can get the royal treatment. But let's start with the simple value of staying in a hotel for a couple of days. Is it really worth it?

The quick answer is no. Paying to stay in a hotel in the same city as your own bed is ridiculous. It's a waste of money, and isn't saving money the main reason you're taking a staycation?

Hard to argue with that. But. . . .

Remember that, with a staycation, you're trying to create mental distance from your everyday routine. By staying for a few days at any kind of hotel, the Fleabagger and the No-Tell Motel being exceptions, you help create the vacation environment. There is no temptation to slip into the home office for a few minutes or to start working on a household project. There is no cleaning the bathroom, making the bed, or fixing breakfast. And with so many hotels to choose from, you don't get pinched with the tourist-trap rates.

I know a lot of people won't agree with me on the hometown hotel idea. Do what's best for you and spend the money on the things that are most important, but at least consider it for a day or two. The hotel will get you away from home and serve as a launching pad for your day of activities. It's great if you're going to a local water park or amusement park, or on a day hike, or maybe off to the spa.

Or if you just want to lie around.

"Sometimes it's just lying in a hotel room and ordering room service and not having to do anything," said Nikki M., who likes to take short staycations at local hotels with her husband, Donald. "It depends on what you want. Sometimes we just want to get away from the laundry and everything."

Now let's get a taste of the pampered lifestyle. We're off to the spa.

Finding Inexpensive Spa Services

Not being a massage expert, or an expert at anything, really, I decided to look into the prices of spa services while writing this book. My findings for the resort spas, in one word, was "Wow." I found one-hour facials for $150, and that was before tax and tip. A sixty-minute massage at the resort and high-end spas was about the same price. Day packages featuring three treatments were $400 and up.

Hey, if you've got the money, go for it. But if you're looking for pampering on a budget, you have alternatives. Independent massage centers are much less expensive than services at spas, and in the last few years, a national massage chain called Massage Envy (*www.massageenvy.com*) has opened more than 750 locations across the country. Prices vary, but the independent massage centers and Massage Envy will probably be less than half the price than at a resort. Maybe $50 for an hour massage, and as I wrote this, Massage Envy was offering an introductory rate of $39 for an hour.

Most of the lower-cost massage centers only do massages, so it's more difficult to find lower-cost options for spa treatments such as a facial, body wrap, or salt scrub. It's especially difficult for me, because I don't understand most of the services on a spa menu. Exfoliating Body Polish? Himalayan Rejuvenation Treatment? Papaya Pineapple Grape Seed Body Scrub?

If you're looking for a full spa treatment, department stores such as Dillard's and JCPenney are less expensive and offer the most popular spa treatments such as massages, manicures, pedicures, facials, and body scrubs. The department stores are often anchor stores for malls, which creates an easy way to have, in my wife's words, the "girls' day out," with lunch, shopping, and some pampering at the spa.

An easy way to locate a spa in your area is at *www.spafinder.com*. Some spas have prices and descriptions of services on their websites, but for others you'll have to call ahead. One note of caution: If it's a small, inexpensive spa, try to find someone who has been there and gives it a good review.

With a little planning, you can create the resort feel without the resort price. Stay at a reasonable hotel, get an hour massage for about fifty bucks, and you'll still have money for a nice dinner at a restaurant you've been wanting to try. Then head back to the hotel and lounge by the pool. Your day probably won't include Ocean Fossil Mineral Therapy or Inner Peace Hypnotic Tranquility Immersion, but you'll feel pampered, and most important, like you're on vacation.

"When you're on a massage table, you don't care if it's Cancun or Dallas," Nikki M. said. "The money you save from traveling you can spend at the spa."

Staycationer Carrie S. echoes that after her stay at a resort near her home.

"We had a nice room, the pool and spa, and all the guest amenities," she said. "We were treated like royalty and felt pampered and spoiled the whole time we were there."

Pampering on an Even Tighter Budget

"Massage school." Yes, it does sound like a late-night show on cable. But if you want to experience the pampered life and your budget is tight, massage schools are an option. Massage schools offer services to the public for about half the price, with a student, supervised by an instructor, giving the massage. Don't worry, these are advanced students giving the massage, not somebody in Rubdowns 101 or an actor researching a role in *Massage School Part III*. It's no frills, but worth a try. You can find links to schools at *www.massageregister.com.*

Along the same lines, beauty schools offer low-cost salon services to the public. Services include haircuts, styling, coloring, scalp treatments, facials, manicures, pedicures, and makeup applications. You can find a list of schools at *www.beautyschoolsdirectory.com.*

Another idea is to create a spa experience at home. At *www
.spaindex.com*, you'll find ingredients and directions for doing
your own facials, body scrubs, baths, and scalp and hair treatments including a "Beer Hair Rinse." It's been at least five years
since I've had enough hair to do any kind of rinse, but a beer hair
rinse does sound manly. (If you're a man, let's do an unnecessary
high five or fist bump here.)

These are the really cheap ways to find some luxury during your
staycation. Maybe too cheap, considering one of the staycation
rules was "treat yourself," which includes not focusing on being
frugal. But I decided to include the massage and beauty schools
and home spa because each staycation budget will be different. And
any time you can save some money on one part of your staycation,
you'll have more to apply to another part.

For example, if you wanted to spend some money on a personal
trainer.

The Fitness Staycation

Resorts and spas often cater to the vacationer trying to get in shape
by offering body analysis and consultation with nutritionists and
exercise physiologists. A less expensive, more staycation-friendly
way to do that is through health clubs.

If you're already a member of a club, you may have access to personal trainers, body analysis testing, and nutritional coaching. If
you're not, a staycation can be a great time to try a fitness program
without a long commitment. Most of the fitness chains such as 24-
hour Fitness and Bally Total Fitness offer seven-day passes, and if

Staycation Reward: The Pampered Life

Resorts and spas are overpriced. So is just about anything associated with luxury. But if a day of indulgence at a spa is what
you've been longing to experience, you can make it work with
your staycation reward.

Many spas offer one-day treatment packages that include two
or three services such as a facial, massage, and body wrap.
The treatment packages will cost you $500 or more, so they're
definitely an extravagance.

Two or three nights at a nice hotel or resort in town is another
way to use your staycation reward, even if you don't use the
spa services. You could also reward yourself with visits to
upscale restaurants, or maybe your staycation will be a chance
to update your wardrobe. You can sell some clothes at a
garage sale or a resale shop, and then take the money you get,
add in your staycation reward, and go on a clothing shopping
spree.

there isn't a free tryout period, you can pay a fee to try the club for a day or week. Health clubs are everywhere, and you can find one near you at *www.healthclubs.com*.

Some clubs are so big that they are like resorts, with saunas, hot tubs, restaurants, and spa services, and all clubs have personal trainers. If there is a Lifetime Fitness near you, getting a week's pass there is great, especially if you have kids who like waterslides (find locations at *www.lifetimefitness.com*).

Gyms can have classes in aerobics, Pilates, cardio kickboxing and "spinning," which is a class on stationary bikes, and some have rock-climbing walls for kids and adults. Visit a club, attend a class, and do what you normally do on a vacation: Try something new.

Staying with that idea, a staycation might be a good time to try yoga. Yoga camps, retreats, and vacations are popular, but you can just stick a toe in the water by finding a yoga class through *www.yogaalliance.com*. You'll learn simple poses such as the Warrior (*Virabhadrasana* in yoga terminology) and the Downward Dog (*Adho Mukha Svanasana*). Most studios will have classes for beginners, so don't worry about being twisted into a human pretzel (Mister Salty Pose).

Ready, Set, Stay

Who knew pampering could be educational? When I was talking to women about ideas for the chapter on resorts and spas, I was introduced to the term *updo*.

A woman can get an updo for a night out, I was told. An up-what?

An *updo* is the term for when hair is pulled up to create a formal look. It's available at salons, and it's an example of a simple way to add a little fun and style to your staycation. My wife also told me that salons offer a "blowout," using a high-powered hair dryer that can help women achieve hairstyles only possible with heated, near-hurricane-force winds. There are also "blow stylists," apparently, but that's probably more than you need to know.

What you need to know from this chapter, more than anything, is that simple is best. Staycationer Brenda told me about her week of going to the movies, pool parties, and visiting restaurants she had never been to before. She and her daughter created a "Mom and Me Day" that included pedicures, getting their hair cut, and watching chick flicks. Although Brenda's husband and son were invited to join, "they seemed less than enthused," Brenda said. So Dad and son countered with a day of fishing. Great idea.

Simple is best, so wouldn't a simple, luxurious trip to a resort be a great vacation? Sure it would, and there will be another chance for that in the future. For now, however, it's about striving for the resort experience without going there.

But having said that, if your budget allows it, and you can

HOME IS WHERE THE LOOK IS

If you normally wouldn't pay for a salt scrub or a facial, now you can treat yourself. If you've always wanted to color your hair or get highlights or extensions, this is your chance. If you've thought about changing your makeup, department stores give free makeovers at their makeup counters. If you want a completely new hairstyle, you've got some money to spend. And then head to the tanning salon for a mist or airbrush tan. When coworkers see your tan and ask, "Where have you been?" tell them it's your "staycation glow."

get a good rate at a resort hotel in your hometown, book it. Plan the staycation well in advance and stay during the nonpeak season and you can get a more affordable rate. Hotel reservations are refundable in most cases, so there's no risk, and if you stay at a resort in your hometown, you're still saving on gas or airfare. Then you can leave the hotel for less expensive spa treatments.

That brings the pampering chapter to a close. It's a bit of a relief for me because body wraps, massages, facials, and anything that includes the word *detoxifying* are not things I know a lot about. But the next chapter moves us into the world of sports, and I'll be happy to tell you about that.

Right after I get my nails done.

Help on the Net

- *www.spafinder.com*: Links to spas nationwide
- *www.spaindex.com*: Ingredients and instructions for home spa treatments
- *www.healthclubs.com*: Links to health clubs nationwide
- *www.massageenvy.com*: Links to Massage Envy locations
- *www.massageregister.com*: List of massage schools by zip code
- *www.beautyschoolsdirectory.com*: Links to beauty schools nationwide
- *www.yogaalliance.com*: List of yoga studios and instructors nationwide
- *www.resortsandlodges.com*: List of world resorts by type and location

Quiz

Would you like to know how to get your family VIP treatment at a sporting event?

Would you like to know how to find minor-league sports teams and learn why they usually offer major-league entertainment?

Does it sound fun to tour a stadium's press box and suites, see a pro team's locker room, and walk out onto the field like a player?

Would you like to spend your staycation lowering your golf handicap, raising your tennis profile, or learning another sport?

Would you like to surprise your kids by signing them up for a pro athlete's sports camp?

If you answered "yes" to any of the above, you'll find ideas in "Sports Staycations" to make your time off a hit.

Chapter 7
Sports Staycations

As Vince Lombardi, legendary coach of the Green Bay Packers once said, "Winning isn't everything, it's the only thing."

Coach Lombardi would get a lot of agreement from diehard sports fans. I've covered a lot of sporting events in my years in journalism, and fans can be crazy. But I've found few things bring out the passion in people—the good and bad passion in people—like an exciting, hard-nosed, hotly contested game of tee ball.

Yes, teeball. I couldn't believe the adrenaline running through the veins of spectators watching a game that included kids who tried to throw the ball with their gloves and ran the bases while flapping their arms. I don't think we were even keeping score, but some people were really screaming out there.

I, on the other hand, couldn't take it too seriously as I watched my son pretend to be a train as he ran the bases and dug his feet into the dirt to create as much dust as possible. He later asked me, as a ball was rolling toward him, if he could use his glove to pick up dirt like Scoop the Backhoe on *Bob the Builder*.

Fortunately, his coach wasn't from the Vince Lombardi school of coaching. He knew not to take sports too seriously, and I'm the same way. That was pretty much a necessity as I grew up playing baseball and basketball and realized I wasn't that great at either.

Despite that, however, I love sports. And because sports are so big in this country, it's easy to put together a sports-themed staycation. Whether you're watching or playing, whether you've got deep pockets or a tight budget, sports can be a big part of your staycation.

Sporting Events

My parents never had season tickets, but as a kid I went to a fair amount of professional and college sporting events. I remember the fun, the excitement, and the feeling of awe I had as I watched the athletes. What I don't remember, on any trip to a game, were fireworks being part of the show. Not when starting lineups were announced in football, not when there was a home run in baseball, not even when my beloved Phoenix Suns achieved a rare feat of beating Kareem Abdul-Jabbar and the Los Angeles Lakers.

But these days, fireworks are as common at sporting events as overdramatic announcers. Fireworks aren't the reason to go to sporting events, but they're a good example of the huge productions that sporting events have become. Teams know that to draw big crowds, they must attract both diehard fans and those who don't know much about the game. That's why most teams now have a member of their staff dedicated to "game presentation," which has nothing to do with the game on the floor, field, or ice. Directors of game presentation coordinate the music and dancers, the interactive games with the crowd, and schedule performers such as jugglers and acrobats. Teams like to call it the "total entertainment experience."

If you want to make attending sporting events a central part of your staycation, check your hometown team's schedule ahead of time. Most vacations are taken during the summer, which works out well because baseball teams play nearly every day and they schedule in blocks of home and away games. A team's homestand can last up to two weeks.

No matter what sporting event you choose, look into special packages for seats, food, and souvenirs. Some teams offer a ticket that includes food and a souvenir, such as a hat, shirt, or poster. I've even seen a ticket that includes all-you-can-eat hot dogs and nachos. (Of course, when you've finished off three plates of nachos, this might not be such a good thing.) The special packages are especially good for families because the kids will want food and they will want a hat, shirt, pennant, or crazy noisemaker. During a staycation, maybe they can choose more than one.

Many stadiums also have sections set aside for families. If you're concerned about the rowdy fans who have made too many trips to the beer line, a family section is a good option.

YOU CAN TAKE IT WITH YOU

Getting autographs is a fun part of attending a professional sports event, but you probably won't get one if you don't bring a pen. That sounds obvious, but many fans who would love to get an autograph from a player aren't prepared when the opportunity arises. Athletes don't carry around permanent markers, and you shouldn't expect another fan to lend you one. The best strategy for getting an autograph is to bring a pen and a glossy photo to be signed, and then to be respectful by addressing the athlete as "Mr." or "Ms." Also, if you want a jersey signed, don't just bring it, wear it. That will make you look more like a true fan than a memorabilia dealer seeking an autograph for profit.

Minor Leagues, Major Fun

MLB (baseball), NBA (basketball), NFL (football), NHL (hockey), MLS (soccer) . . . there's an alphabet soup of elite-level sporting events from which to choose. But not every staycationer will have the major leagues in his or her hometown. No problem. Check into the minor and developmental leagues and you'll still have fun. Maybe even more.

Minor league baseball is sometimes better than the majors because it's less expensive and you can get seats closer to the action. It's also likely that a minor league baseball team is close to you, because there are so many levels from Class A to Triple-A, as well as independent leagues and summer leagues for college baseball players. Minor league teams are also very fan-friendly, which we'll talk more about below. You can find links to team websites at *www.minorleaguebaseball.com*.

Another great summer sports event, especially if you have daughters, is the Women's National Basketball Association (*www.wnba.com*). This is the majors for women's basketball, but I put it in this section because it's so overshadowed by the NBA. The WNBA isn't quite the spectacle of the NBA, but the game presentation is very good and the tickets are priced right. The same is true at most minor league sporting events.

Minor league hockey teams are also all over the country, with names such as the Grand

KIDS AND SPORTING EVENTS

If you want to watch every play of a game and not miss the dramatic ending, don't bring your kids. They won't sit still for nine innings or four quarters, and they'll want you to explain everything to them. Find a babysitter and save yourself the frustration. If you do bring your kids, however, you might be as entertained by them as the game. The first time I took my oldest son to a baseball game, he was four years old. We left the game early, so I don't know who won, but I didn't care. Neither did Ryan, but he did talk about the game for months. That's what makes sports a winner, even when your team loses.

Rapids Griffins and the Bossier-Shreveport MudBugs. They play a season from early fall to late spring in several minor league hockey organizations, all of which have websites with links to their teams.

You might also have a junior hockey team in your area and not know it. Junior hockey, a skill-development program of USA hockey, puts on a good show. It features several levels of teams with players ages twenty and under who are hoping to land college scholarships or get drafted by an NHL team. It was created for players looking for more of a challenge than what they can get through a high school team. You'll find the typical minor league fun at the games with mascots, games for the fans, music, and other entertainment, and you'll find all the teams at *www.usajuniorhockey.com.*

One more sport to check out is arena football. Two leagues, the AFL and the AFL2, play seasons that start a few weeks after the Super Bowl and stretch into early summer. Arena football is a rock-and-roll, highly caffeinated version of football that appeals to the Mountain Dew demographic. "Total entertainment experience" is actually part of the AFL's mission statement.

The minor league sports that are available depend on the time of year when you take your staycation. They're lots of fun, and if you have kids, they can probably get autographs from the players. Unlike at major league games, that's a thrill for the kids *and* the players.

Now let's talk about how to make the games more special.

Getting the Special Treatment

You're on staycation time, so any trip to a sporting event shouldn't be rushed. Get to the game early, watch the players warm up, and you can get autographs. Stay late and you might be able to get more (and avoid traffic). And here's something many people don't know about: You can contact a team's front office or community relations department and ask for VIP treatment. No, they won't send a limo to pick you up or roll out a red carpet, but you can get special attention. This is especially true in the minor leagues, whether it's baseball, hockey, football, or basketball. Minor league teams are very eager to please.

So take advantage of that. Before you go to a game, contact the team's front office or community relations department. Tell them you're coming out to a game and you want to know how you can make it more special. If you're bringing kids to the game, definitely tell the team that.

You and your family could be part of a promotion or skit. The team might also allow your kids to get on the field for part of batting practice or give them a chance to run the bases between innings or after the game. Maybe your kids will get to sit in the dugout for a few minutes before the game or have the chance to meet some of the players, get autographs, and take pictures with them. Whether a pro athlete is destined for the Hall of Fame or the end of the bench, meeting him or her is a thrill for kids.

A team might not be able to set something up for that night, so again, planning ahead is valuable. But it's hard to imagine many teams saying, "Sorry, we can't do anything for you." That would be like saying, "Why don't you just go find somewhere else to spend your money."

That's why it never hurts to ask.

One last thing, as we finish discussing how someone else can make a sporting event more special. You can do it, too, especially if you have young kids. If you're going to a minor league game, make it a major league event by immersing yourself in it. Stop by the team shop and get a team shirt and a team hat. If your kids want to make signs for the game, encourage them (and maybe help with spelling). Take pictures during the game of the kids in their seats, with their sports garb on, and as they eat treats from the concession stand. It shows the kids that the staycation is a special time. A vacation time.

Stadium Tours

Many people don't take advantage of stadium tours, but it's probably because they don't know they are available. Most stadiums and arenas used for pro sports offer them, and they are absolutely awesome for kids. For adults, too. What sports fan, at any age, wouldn't be thrilled to walk on the field or court of a pro team?

A good example is the Meadowlands Experience Tour in East Rutherford, New Jersey, which includes a behind-the-scenes look at the Izod Center, where the New Jersey Nets play, and Giants Stadium, where the New York Giants and Jets play. The tour of Giants Stadium includes a chance to go into the press box, check out a luxury suite, and see the Jets' locker room. A tour guide will also take you through the tunnel the players use to walk onto the field that has been home to football and soccer games, as well as some of the most famous concerts ever, since it opened in 1976. If you bring a football for the tour, you can even have friends take a picture of you catching a pass.

At Wrigley Field in Chicago, fans can tour a ballpark that has been open for nearly a century. It's the site of Babe Ruth's famous "called shot" in the 1932 World Series, when he allegedly pointed to a spot in the bleachers before hitting a home run. The ninety-minute tour includes the Cubs' Clubhouse, the press box, the visitor's clubhouse, bleachers, dugouts, and the opportunity to step onto the field.

You'll probably find a similar stadium or arena tour in your area. There's a charge for tours at most stadiums, but not an outrageous price. As with the factory tours, the stadium tours provide an opportunity to take advantage of a company's desire to boost its public image (and in this case, help you forget that you'll pay five bucks for a hot dog on game day). All you need to do is check a team's website or call its administrative offices.

It will make you feel closer to the team, as with staycationer couple Brenda and Ed, who toured the locker room of the Dallas Stars hockey team.

Ed's one-word description: "Wow."

Brenda's: "Stinky."

It's Your Turn to Play

Now that you've seen the experts of the game, get some expert help on yours. If you're a golfer or a tennis player, or just want to try out those sports, it's easy to find group lessons or one-on-one instruction. Municipal golf courses and tennis clubs, public and private, offer professional lessons.

Even if you've never played a sport, it's amazing what can be done in a week's worth of coaching sessions. For tennis, simply call up a local tennis club and ask about lessons or search the database at *www.usptafindapro.com*, which is provided by the U.S.

Pro Tennis Association. Those interested in golfing can find a pro at *www.pgapros.com*. You might be able to take a lesson with your spouse, a friend, or your kids.

Lessons for Kids

Speaking of kids, sport lessons are really easy to find for them. Golf and tennis clubs offer lessons, of course, but kids can get instruction in virtually every sport. Check for class offerings through the parks and recreation department in your city, and nearby cities, which usually offer classes to nonresidents at a slightly higher fee. You can also find links to day camps for sports as varied as cheerleading, diving, martial arts, and skateboarding at *www.kidscamps.com*.

Sports camps offered by pro teams and pro athletes are also a big thrill for kids. Some can be expensive, but day camps usually are not. And although it's not always a good thing, kids are pretty much in awe of pro athletes. Your kids will have lots of fun and improve their skills at the camps, which are generally run through a pro team's community relations department. Call the team's front office to find out dates, times, and how to sign up. You can also check a team's website or call the front office to find out when athletes are making special appearances in your community.

Ready, Set, Stay

This chapter started with a quote from Vince Lombardi that, as I was growing up, I would've agreed with. I played to win back then.

Staycation Reward: Sports Staycation

No matter where you sit at a sporting event, it's going to be fun. But if you want to make it more exciting, use your staycation reward to land some really good seats. It's a completely different experience than watching the game from high in the stands. If your staycation will be in the summer, try getting seats next to the dugout for a baseball game. You'll actually be able to hear some of the players talking in front of the dugout and hear the pop of the catcher's mitt on a fastball. Just watch out for foul balls.

You may not be able to afford to buy those pricey tickets regularly, and it may not be worth it if you go to a lot of games. But for a sports fan, it's something to experience at least once. Sometimes you can get the tickets for prime seats directly from the team's box office, but it's more likely that you'll need a ticket service. If you search the Internet for your team's name and "tickets," you'll find lots of ticket brokers.

You can also use your staycation reward to load up on sports apparel or buy a tennis racket, golf clubs, or other equipment. That frivolous sports collectible you want? Maybe it's a rare rookie card, an autographed photo, or a pair of cleats worn by a football star. Or maybe it's the mouth guard LeBron James used in a game, which was once sold for $1,500. Whatever the collectible is, the staycation reward might be your chance to get it.

HOME IS WHERE THE FAN IS

You don't have to spend big money to enjoy a sports collectibles shop. Just browsing for an hour or two at several shops can be a fun part of a staycation, and if you find a sports collectibles show, you can spend a whole day looking at history. Check *www.upcomingcardshows .com* and you might find one in your area. The shows often have pro athletes signing autographs (sometimes for a fee, depending on his or her popularity). It's another way to add sports to your staycation. And even if you don't know whether Joe Montana was a quarterback or a centerfielder, collectibles shops are fun. They generally have a lot of memorabilia unrelated to sports, too.

So did my younger brother, which is probably why so many of our video-game battles ended as wrestling matches. But now that I'm older, I prefer the well-known sports philosophy of "it's not whether you win or lose, it's how you play the game."

It applies to sports and staycations. If you were winning this vacation game, you'd probably be cruising in the Caribbean, zigzagging across Europe, or dropping loads of cash somewhere. But what you need to do is play the staycation game the right way.

If you like to golf, use the time off to play a different course each day of your staycation. Make one of those courses at a resort, spend a night there, and get a lesson from one of the club's pros. Then spend some of the money you've saved by forgoing the traditional vacation to buy a golf club you want to add to your bag. Tennis fans can do something similar with lessons, a new racquet, and getting some court time during a stay at a resort. After all, a staycation doesn't have to be cheap. Just cheaper than the traditional vacation.

For those who do need to pull in the reins on the budget, there are sporting events to attend, stadiums to tour, local sports museums, and halls of fame. (If you search "list of halls and walks of fame" on *www.wikipedia.org*, you'll find hundreds of state and regional sports halls of fame.) And if you just want to take it easy, going to a sports bar and grill for a night of eating, drinking, and watching sports on a dozen televisions can be a highlight. One of the advantages a staycation has over a traditional vacation is simplicity, so why not?

Help on the Net

- *www.minorleaguebaseball.com*: Links to all levels of minor league baseball teams
- *www.wnba.com*: Home of Women's National Basketball Association, with links to teams
- *www.usajuniorhockey.com*: Links to all levels of junior hockey
- *www.arenafootball.com*: Home of Arena Football League, with links to teams
- *www.af2.com*: Home of Arena Football 2, with links to teams
- *www.usptafindapro.com*: Links to tennis professionals who give lessons
- *www.pgapros.com*: Links to golf professionals who give lessons
- *www.tennisresortsonline.com*: Links to resorts offering tennis
- *www.kidscamps.com*: List and information on sports camps for kids
- *www.upcomingcardshows.com*: Calendar and information on upcoming sports collectibles shows

Quiz

Do you enjoy live theater or have you ever wanted to get involved in the production of a community play?

Would you be interested in attending a concert with big names but not big prices?

Could a festival with music, food, art, shopping, carnival rides, and souvenir T-shirts be a fun part of your staycation?

Would you like to make a movie experience more exciting, find a drive-in theater nearby, or know how to thrill your kids with a "Backyard Movie Night"?

Would you like to find a good comedy club and learn how *you* can be part of the show?

If you answered "yes" to any of the above, you'll find ideas in "Movies, Plays, and Other Entertainment" to make your staycation top the charts.

Chapter 8

Movies, Plays, and Other Entertainment

In college, I took a class called "Theater Appreciation." I took it because I heard it was an easy class to ace, and yes, it was.

But I did learn a lot, and the highlight of the class was an assignment that I dreaded when I heard about it. I had to work for a week as a stagehand during a community theater production. It turned out to be really exciting, and a lot of fun, as I helped move sets between scenes and place props where they needed to be. That's also when I first realized just how talented people involved in community theater can be.

Community Theater Productions

Fifteen years later, I'm a huge fan of community theater. It also seemed like a great opening topic for a chapter on bringing the arts to a staycation. After all, community theater is inexpensive, it's nearby, and it's something that's often overlooked.

But not by Amy and Kevin, a staycationer couple from Ohio.

"We prefer community theater versus big Broadway," Amy said. "Community theater gives us much more than big Broadway."

Productions at smaller theaters certainly provide more bang for the buck. At a smaller theater, you can actually see the actors and singers instead of thirty rows of heads between you and the stage.

Don't get me wrong. Broadway productions are fantastic. Touring Broadway-like productions are also terrific, so if you can make those part of a staycation, go for it. But don't brush off community theaters, or other small stages, because they're not as polished. They aren't as polished, it's true, but it's not like the actors are going to forget their lines or start laughing in the middle of the play. It's not like a third-grade's Christmas play with shepherds who are dressed in bed sheets and carrying hockey sticks as crooks.

You can find a community theater near you, and its production schedule, in the database at *www.aact.org*, the Internet home of the American Association of Community Theatre.

If you live in a large metro area, there are probably several community theaters presenting shows. Smaller stages, some with professional actors and some with amateurs, are also great destinations. See four shows in four nights, even if it's a dinner theater, and you'll still spend less than for one typical Broadway show.

On the final night, you can check to see if there is a Broadway production touring through your city. To make the evening more special, add dinner out and a night at a hotel. You can also hire people to take pictures as you get out of the limo and then push one away and curse the paparazzi.

Okay, that's probably pushing the creativity too far.

YOU CAN TAKE IT WITH YOU
You might not be able to get great seats for a play or concert, but you can always bring the show closer to you by packing a pair of compact binoculars. Zoom in to see a guitarist strumming, a singer belting out a tune, an actor delivering a dramatic monologue, or maybe just to see how long the line of cars is trying to exit the parking lot. Binoculars can be found for as little as $20 at Wal-Mart, Target, and on the Internet, and they can be used for sporting events and nature hikes. They're also great for kids. Get a pair of kid-sized binoculars and your kids will be entertained even if they don't want to watch the concert or play.

Music Tours

Get out your 1980s concert T-shirt, parachute pants, legwarmers, and fingerless gloves. I just read about the Regeneration Tour, with the Human League, A Flock of Seagulls, Naked Eyes, and Belinda Carlisle putting on a show together. Wow, talk about memories (some embarrassing). I wonder if the movie *Sixteen Candles* played on video screens as a warmup act.

Yes, it's the era of the rock-band reunion show. Boston and REO Speedwagon were touring together in 2008, as were the Steve Miller Band and Joe Cocker. You could find Poison and Dokken on one ticket, Journey touring with Heart and Cheap Trick, and a night of music with Cyndi Lauper, Joan Jett, and the B-52s.

The appeal of the above shows depends a lot on your age and musical taste. But no matter what you're into, you can make concerts a part of your staycation. Sometimes a concert can even be the centerpiece of it, as with staycationer Lin B. She and her husband spent their staycation visiting museums, supporting "mom and pop" restaurants, going to the movies, and spending time

STAYCATION BONUS #3:
HOTEL ANNOYANCES

Staying in a hotel for a couple days of your staycation is a good idea. But hotel annoyances are so numerous, and they are such a popular subject, that they qualify as a Staycation Bonus. At hotels, you may find flat pillows, hotel curtains that allow a thin stream of light into the room, rooms that aren't ready at check-in time, and who knows what else. All are annoying, although in the rare cases when your room isn't available at check-in time, you should ask for a discount. Also ask for a room as far away as possible from the elevator and the ice machine to ensure a peaceful stay.

at a lake near their home. They finished it off by seeing country singer Martina McBride in concert.

"It was a highlight of the entire week," Lin said.

They planned it that way. You can plan ahead the same way by visiting your local newspaper's website and clicking on the entertainment section. Typically there are concert calendars and listings of bars and clubs that have live rock, country, blues, and jazz music. You can also check the travel guides for your area at *www.frommers.com* and *www.fodors.com* and find bars, music clubs, and dance clubs.

City Festivals

More good reasons to plan your staycation ahead of time are city, community, and special-interest festivals. They often have impressive musical lineups that you typically won't find together.

One example is the Rock the Fall Festival at the Blue Mountain Ski Area in Palmerton, Pennsylvania. At the last festival, in addition to the arts and crafts displays, tasty food, and free lift rides, the music lineup included rock groups Everclear, Soul Asylum, and Cracker. Country stars Tracy Lawrence and Terri Clark also performed. A few months earlier, the Jackson Hole Jazz & Heritage Festival in Wyoming had the Black Crowes and Wilco for rock fans, the jazz trio of Medeski Martin & Wood, and the added nostalgia of the Beach Boys' Brian Wilson. Festivals like those are perfect anchors for a fun staycation.

How do you find these festivals? Again, newspaper websites are a great source of information. City governments also post information on their websites about the festivals they organize or host, and I guarantee there are festivals in your area that you don't know about. Type "list of festivals in the United States" into *www.wikipedia.org* and you'll find nature festivals, cultural festivals, science festivals, sports festivals, music festivals, and more.

Food festivals are really great. They often offer art exhibits, music, and lots of activities for kids including carnival games and rides. And they always have food, of course. At *www.foodreference.com*, you'll find links and descriptions for hundreds of them, searchable by location and date. The Maine Lobster Festival, the Virginia Peach Festival, and the Watermelon Festival in Hope, Arkansas, are all there. So is the Weekend of Fire in Fairfield, Ohio, which features spicy foods such as salsas, barbecue sauces, and jalapeños. And to prove there is something for everyone, you can also find information on the 26th Annual Testicle Festival in Clinton, Montana. That festival features servings of deep-fried bull testicles, also known as the "Rocky Mountain Oyster," so it really is a food festival. I can only imagine how many "We're havin' a ball at the Testicle Festival!" T-shirts are sold there each year.

You'll also find several beer festivals, but I'll let you discover more about them. I've already discussed drinking beer after a Coors tour, described a visit to a sake brewery, and later we'll talk about winery tours. I don't want you to get the wrong idea about me. To prove my sobriety, here's another good way to search for festivals in your hometown: Use the database at *www.festivals.com*.

Movies: Adding Extra to the Ordinary

Twenty years ago, when VHS was wiping out Betamax in the videotape format war, movies weren't that easy to rent. Small, independent video stores were everywhere, Blockbuster was just starting to grow, and there were long waiting lists to rent movies. I remember my family was on a waiting list for several weeks to rent *Revenge of the Nerds* (showing our very questionable taste in movies).

Now, video stores are everywhere, it's cheap to buy videos, and Netflix and Blockbuster offer services that mail movie rentals directly to your home. Memberships are as low as five bucks per month. Video kiosks can also be found in grocery stores with the latest releases, making renting a movie as easy as getting a snack from a vending machine. Even easier, in fact, because the movies never get stuck coming out like candy bars sometimes do.

So renting movies is more convenient than ever. That's a good thing, but the convenience has made watching a movie, which was once a special experience, commonplace. Kind of mundane.

Still, simply catching up on movies you missed over the last year might be a fun way to spend your staycation. You could also use the time to get into one of the television series you missed. Netflix and Blockbuster allow you to rent a season's worth of episodes, and they give you access to movies that are often hard to find in stores, such as old classics, independent films, and documentaries. You can also find movies that will help you feel like you're traveling. Search "scenic travel movies" and you'll find several lists of top travel movies with selections such as *Lawrence of Arabia* and *Under the Tuscan Sun.*

I know some people who, in the weeks before the Academy Awards, rent all the best-picture nominees so they can decide for themselves. They don't do it as part of a staycation, but it would seem to fit. You can reserve the films nominated for best picture, or pick a category such as best actor or actress, and then be a critic.

You'll create your own Academy Awards, and perhaps a lively discussion with your staycation partner. Especially if your choice for best picture stars Adam Sandler or has a character named Borat.

As with all staycation activities, the key is making it stand out from the ordinary.

THE BACKYARD THEATER

Drive-in theaters peaked in the 1960s but very few remain today. So if you can find one in your area, it's a cool nostalgia trip for a staycation. And if there isn't a drive-in nearby, you can create the experience in your backyard. All you need is a computer with a DVD player, a white wall or bed sheet to use as the movie screen, and a projector, which you can find by doing an Internet search for "projector rental" and your city. Stores that rent audiovisual equipment for business meetings will have basic projectors for about $100 a day or weekend. If you tell them what your plans are, they can make sure it will work. They also rent projection screens if you want one. Plug some small speakers in to your computer, get out some folding chairs, and enjoy a classic double feature in your backyard.

"If we're going to watch a movie, we're going to pop popcorn and make it special," said Joslyn T., who has two daughters. "We're going to make it something more than just popping in a video."

Tom and Laura did something similar during their staycation. In the middle of a warm summer afternoon in Florida, they closed the curtains and darkened the house to watch *Phantom of the Opera*.

"That's her favorite movie, and she wanted that romantic atmosphere," Tom said. "It turned it into like a real movie experience."

Tom said he would've preferred a movie like *Gladiator*, but for any vacation, traditional or stay-at-home, compromise is important. So, too, is making the most of your time off. So if you're watching a movie at home, pop popcorn, get the movie-sized box of candy that you like at the store, and darken the room. Make it feel like you're at the theater.

Or you can just go to the theater, of course. Even with all the conveniences of home and new high-definition televisions that look great, I think I'll always prefer going to the theater. And if I can find enough movies I want to see during a staycation, I wouldn't mind heading to a movie theater, and a different restaurant, each night of the week.

Comedy Clubs and Open-Mike Night

Today's most famous comedians such as Jerry Seinfeld and Ellen DeGeneres still do comedy tours. They're great live, but they perform at huge venues, which aren't the best settings for comedy.

You can have more fun during trips to smaller comedy clubs. Some comedians are great, some aren't so great, but they are always interesting. And it's a fun change of pace from a night at the movies or a nightclub. If you don't know if there's a comedy club in your area, you can find a list of clubs at *www.chucklemonkey.com*.

Open-mike nights are also fun, and less expensive, at comedy clubs. Open-mike is often during the middle of the week and serves as an audition for a spot in the weekend lineup of comics that warm up the stage for a headliner. It's fun to watch, but if you're talented and brave, you can get up on stage for a few minutes. Many comedy clubs also offer comedy workshops that give people lessons in performing standup comedy, so maybe your staycation could be the first step toward getting discovered.

Staycation Reward: Entertainment Staycations

Here's the chance to get that new television you want. Make it part of a week of renting movies and your staycation reward can really make it special.

No, I'm not providing an excuse to spend $3,000 on a new plasma television. It has to be within reason. If you're taking a staycation to save $2,000 on a traditional vacation, then buying a $3,000 television doesn't make any sense.

But a new television, portable DVD player, stereo equipment, or iPod is a nice reward for taking a staycation. Another possibility is a new video camera, which will help you capture memories of your staycation. One tip on saving money on electronic purchases is to look into buying the floor models (the equipment that is on display in the store). Yes, there may be a scratch on the DVD player or the television might not be the color you want, but you can save a lot of money on these lightly used models.

Other ways to splurge include front-row tickets for a concert or the theater, which you can find through online ticket brokers (search "ticket brokers") and sites that allow ticket buyers to resell their tickets, such as *www.stubhub.com*, *www.craigslist.com*, and *www.ebay.com*. You can also get first choice of tickets for many concerts by joining the "frequent listener" club for your favorite radio station, which you can usually sign up for online. The stations often sponsor concerts and give the listeners a chance to buy tickets before they're sold to the general public.

You can also use your staycation reward to buy a few CDs or expand your library of downloaded music. Or if you want to improve your television options, try upgrading your cable or satellite service to a better package of channels for six months or a year. Here's a hint regarding that: If you call a cable or satellite service and say you're considering switching to another provider, you can sometimes get a reduced rate on upgrades.

HOME IS WHERE THE STAGE IS

Whether there's a big stage, small stage, or barely a stage at all, theaters provide great plays to watch. They also offer great plays to be a part of. If you want to be an usher, sew costumes, take tickets, work with lighting and sound, do makeup, or be a stage manager, you will be greeted with open arms at a community theater. And if you want to be an actor . . . well, the theater will still want you. Without volunteers, community theaters wouldn't exist. You don't need to take a week or two off from work to help prepare for a play, but volunteering at a community theater fits well with a staycation. You'll be trying something different, meeting new people, and having a great time. Those are three things that add up to a great vacation.

Or you can just watch. That's much more relaxing.

Open-mike nights aren't just at comedy clubs. Other bars and clubs open up the microphone to wannabe singers, storytellers, and poets. You'll see some people with real talent who haven't been discovered. You'll also see some people like the character Phoebe on *Friends* who clumsily strummed a guitar while singing "Smelly Cat." Either way, very entertaining.

You can find an open-mike night near you at *www.open mikes.org*. A list of poetry slams, a competition where authors read their works and judges vote for their favorite, is at *www .poetryslam.com*.

Ready, Set, Stay

Famous director Alfred Hitchcock once said that a good movie is "when the price of the admission, the dinner and the babysitter was well worth it." He also said the length of a movie should be directly related to the endurance of the human bladder, so the guy knew movies.

Americans certainly know movies well. A movie is our favorite two-hour escape from reality, whether in a theater or at home, and even bad movies pull in big dollars. It's the entertainment we fall back on when we don't know what else to do.

If you're a big movie fan, maybe all you need for a staycation is a rental membership and a nice television setup. But during a staycation, consider doing something more. Tour different movie theaters in your area and see an IMAX film. Go to a smaller theater and see an independent film or documentary, and visit an historic theater in your area if there is one. You can find links to historic and restored theaters at *www.cinematreasures.org*.

If you really want a classic, and somewhat bizarre, movie experience, the *Rocky Horror Picture Show* is still showing at nearly 100 theaters in the United States. The typical showtime is midnight on a Friday or Saturday, and you can find times and locations at *www.rockyhorror.com*. You might even be able to schedule your staycation around one of the dozens of film festivals each year across the country.

Plays are also great entertainment, no matter what size the theater company. Dinner theaters are a fun twist, and some restaurants offer nights with dinner and an interactive murder mystery play. And have you ever heard of "environmental theater"? No, it doesn't involve Al Gore or melting icecaps. Environmental theater is a style of theater that is staged in a real-world setting instead of a playhouse and immerses the crowd in the show. A good example is *Tony n' Tina's Wedding*, a comedy that has been around for twenty years, and is usually playing in a dozen U.S. cities at the same time. Audience members are guests at the wedding, and a wedding-day disaster unfolds around them. It was one of the funniest shows I've ever seen. You can find dates and locations at *www .tonylovestina.com*.

One last thing about plays: If you want to try acting, some small theater companies offer acting workshops. It could be a fun family activity, and your child might discover a love for acting. Or maybe just a way to be more dramatic when you ask him or her to take out the trash.

You could also try attending a symphony once. Don't worry, you don't have to wear a tuxedo or evening gown. Some people like to dress up, but most people will dress somewhere between business casual and business formal. You can also explore variety in music by checking out a different nightclub each night. There's even (gasp!) Karaoke Night.

Come on, it might be fun. Take a brewery tour first and maybe you'll have the guts to try the high notes on "Dream Weaver."

Help on the Net

- *www.aact.org*: American Association of Community Theatre, searchable database of companies
- *www.foodreference.com*: Links to food festivals, searchable by area or date
- *www.festivals.com*: Searchable database of festivals
- *www.blockbuster.com, www.netflix.com*: Online video rental services
- *www.chucklemonkey.com*: List and links to comedy clubs
- *www.openmikes.org*: Listings for clubs with open-mike nights
- *www.poetryslam.com*: Listings for poetry slams, with descriptions
- *www.cinematreasures.org*: Information and links for historic movie theaters
- *www.rockyhorror.com*: Home page for cult classic *The Rocky Horror Picture Show*
- *www.tonylovestina.com*: Home page for long-running interactive play, *Tony n' Tina's Wedding*

Would you like to relax on a sunset cruise by sipping wine and listening to waves gently crashing against the side of a boat?

Do you want to spend more time alone with your loved one but can't find the right babysitter for the kids?

Would you like to take a scenic train ride that includes dinner and live music?

Do you think that camping can be romantic?

Would you like to tour a winery, take a class in couples massage, or learn other simple ways to be romantic?

If you answered "yes" to any of the above, you'll find ideas in "Romantic Staycations" to take to heart.

Chapter 9
Romantic
Staycations

When you add kids to your life, you add great joy and tremendous responsibility. You also add the kind of painful financial multiplication that can put the squeeze on a big vacation.

It's the same with romance. Once you have kids, everything changes. If you're a parent of young kids, you might even be thinking,

"A chapter on romance? How short is this going to be?"

Well, it could be very short. Kids, God bless 'em, are an unbelievable drain on a parent's time and energy. I don't regret for a moment having my two sons, but by the time I come home from work, listen to the kids say "Watch this! Watch this!" fifty times, and spend an hour as a Daddy jungle gym . . .

Wait a second. My wife just reminded me that we have three sons. As I said, kids are a drain on a parent's time, energy, and mental acuity.

Anyway, romance takes a hit when you have kids. But relationship experts talk about the importance of romance in a healthy marriage, and that couples need to make time for it. That's something you'll have during your staycation, so make the most of it.

We'll start by removing the first hurdle: the kids. If you don't have kids, you can skip over the first section and jump in on "Day Cruises and In-Town Getaways."

Getting Some Alone Time

Complimenting your spouse is a romantic idea, so I'll start with this:

My wife is a wonderful mom. I'm very lucky that she's an expert at nurturing, understanding, and educating children. It allows me to focus on giving piggyback rides and teaching the boys key concepts such as "if you fill the fountain-drink cup all the way to the top, when you place the lid on and put the straw in, the cup will overflow."

Having said all that, I'll move on to this:

My wife is very particular about leaving our kids with a babysitter. She doesn't require a CIA background check, but it's close. So if you or your spouse are the same way, I figured the romance chapter should start with ways to free yourselves from the great blessings and romance killers of your life.

First of all, if you have relatives or friends whom you trust as babysitters, coordinate with them and make sure they are available for a night or two during your staycation. That's what Nancy and Mike did during theirs. They made sure that the nanny who watches their kids when they are at work was available for a full day during their staycation. "So we could get out for a little piece of our vacation," Nancy said.

Nancy and Mike went to a Japanese steakhouse that they had decided to try when they could find the time alone. A staycation gave them the chance to arrange that time, and they still had plenty of time off to spend with their kids.

If you don't know someone who can babysit, you can ask friends for leads. Just make it clear that you're not trying to "steal" their sitter. You can also search for a babysitter at national sitter services such as *www.4sitters.com*, *www.sittercity.com*, and *www.seekingstters.com*, which have bios and links to potential sitters.

YOU CAN TAKE IT WITH YOU

A night out, or in, can be made more special with some romantic mementos. If you're driving to a dinner, bring along a CD, or load up the mp3 player, with songs that represent the special times in your relationship. If you go camping, take a portable DVD player and the video of your wedding or other family videos. Another idea is to write love letters that you present to each other during your time together. Don't worry, you don't have to make the letter a huge, emotional Hallmark moment or write like William Shakespeare. Just include a memory of time spent with your loved one, write the way you speak, and if thou normally speaketh like Shakespeare, seeketh help. For more tips visit www.lovingyou.com.

A membership fee is required for those services, but the website *www.barefootstudent.com* is free and has extensive listings of college students who want to babysit. You can also find local sitter services by searching the Internet for "babysitting service" and your city.

No matter how you find a sitter, it's best to have a face-to-face meeting before hiring him or her. Also ask for references, ask about experience and emergency training, and give the babysitter a tour of your home before the night (or day) out. Babysitters can be expensive, but a good one is worth it.

We all love our kids, but there's probably no better way to break from the everyday than to schedule some time away from them. One night out, for a concert or show, a nice dinner, or just to talk without interruption, is a great way to reconnect with your partner.

That's what the relationship experts say, anyway. I'm not that smart. I just like spending time with my wife.

Day Cruises and In-Town Getaways

Yeah, we're not talking about a seven-day Mediterranean cruise. Or a cruise to the Bahamas, which is what my wife and I took for our honeymoon. It was fantastic, and when conditions are better for dropping a few thousand dollars on a cruise, we might do it again. Maybe just so I can see how many people return home with the Caribbean-style cornrows.

But what makes a cruise so romantic? Is it the starry skies, the sound of the waves crashing against the boat, the feeling of isolation with the one you love? I'm not sure, but you can get some of the cruise feeling with a day cruise. The cruises often last ninety minutes to several hours and are inexpensive. On larger boats, live music is often part of the trip. (Those are lots of fun for kids, too.)

If there's a lake near your home with boat rentals, there's a good chance that dinner cruises, sometimes called "sunset cruises," are available. One example is a sunset cruise that is offered on the Wisconsin Dells, a five-mile stretch on the Wisconsin River. The two-hour trip includes hors d'oeuvres, wine, and then dinner as passengers check out the cliffs, canyons, and rock formations carved into sandstone.

Your local sunset cruise might not offer the same scenery, but it will still be a nice romantic getaway. Some cruises are on larger boats with multiple couples or families, but you can also charter a smaller boat. The best way to find one is to search the Internet for "dinner cruise" or "sunset cruise" and your city or the name of a nearby lake.

To extend your romantic evening, you can check in at a local hotel after the cruise. Some hotels offer specific one-night romantic packages that include a stay in a luxury suite with a Jacuzzi, champagne, dinner in your room, and spa services if available. Staycationers Nikki and Donald have made several one-night getaways, and are planning more. They're not the only ones, Nikki said.

"We were at the hotel pool, and looking around, you could tell that there were other staycationers there," Nikki said. "We kind of laughed about that, but it felt like a true vacation."

Your staycation will also feel like a true vacation if you find a local bed and breakfast. Bed and breakfasts generally have fewer kids around and they cater to couples looking for romance. They have more romantic charm than hotels, and in most cases, they are warm and friendly because the innkeeper usually lives on the premises. You can find a bed and breakfast in your area at *www .bedandbreakfast.com.*

Train Rides

Take a train ride and you'll learn the history of an area and see acres of beautiful scenery. You'll also find a tranquil, cozy setting that makes a train ride the most romantic form of travel. There are also scenic train trips all over the country that make a staycation day feel like a vacation day.

In Arizona, there is the Grand Canyon Railroad that takes passengers from Flagstaff—a city 100 miles north of Phoenix—for a scenic ride to the Canyon and back. On the West Coast, the

Yosemite Mountain Sugar Pine Railroad has vintage trains that travel along a former logging run through the Sierra National Forest in California. And on the East Coast, the Scenic Western Maryland Railroad travels through rugged mountains, over a truss bridge, and completes a hairpin curve. Then it finishes on a railroad turntable that most people only see while helping their kids put together wooden tracks for Thomas the Tank Engine.

Most of the train rides will feature great scenery and offer both climate-controlled and open-air coaches. Tour guides will tell you about the history of the railroad and the surrounding areas, so you can also learn something. But what really makes a train ride perfect for a staycation is that it's so relaxing. The pace is slow, the mood is laid back, and it's a wonderfully mellow experience.

You can find a national directory of scenic train rides, sorted by state, at *www.traintraveling.com*. Check for special packages, too, that include dinner and live music. Some also have Sunday champagne brunches and murder mystery shows that take place

ROMANCE ON THE DANCE FLOOR

Romance doesn't always have to mean something like satin sheets, candles, and poems with words such as *bewitching* and *seraphic*. Just getting to focus on each other and work on something together is romantic. Dance lessons are a good opportunity for that, and even if you'll never be confused with a winner on *Dancing with the Stars*, you will have fun. My wife and I took dance lessons through a class offered by our city's parks and recreation department and had a great time. You can check with your city's parks and recreation department or find a directory of dance schools at *www.ballroomdancers.com*.

during the ride. The Sacramento RiverTrain in California even has a Great Train Robbery ride on Saturdays, which features characters entertaining the passengers and an Old West gunfight (great for kids, obviously, but also fun for two).

Massage Lessons

You've given your significant other many massages over the years, and any massage feels great. But do you really know what you're doing?

If you take a massage class for couples, you will. Massage schools sometimes offer couples classes, as do massage centers and individual massage therapists. You can learn as part of a class or as just a couple, and some instructors will even teach at your home.

If you prefer, you can skip the instructor and head to the library or bookstore for a book on couples massage. Massage videos are also available for sale on the Internet, and they can even be rented through *www.netflix.com* and *www.blockbuster.com*. Just search for massage and—tah-dah!—you have more than a dozen from which to choose.

So here's the plan. Rent a romantic movie and a video on massage lessons for your staycation. Learn the art of massage and then create the spa experience at home with ideas from "The Pampered Life" chapter. And, because this is the adults-only chapter, I'll mention, too, that there are also books and videos available for instruction in "sensual massage."

Stop blushing. We're all adults here. I hope so, anyway. If you're not an adult, please stop reading here and proceed to the

"Especially for Kids" chapter. I'm not kidding. Don't make me give you a timeout.

Camping for Two

Experiencing the great outdoors is a natural aphrodisiac. That's what some people say, anyway. Unfortunately, they might be the "some people" who buy libido-boosting pills sold via e-mail messages that misspell the word *sexual*.

So maybe it's best not to trust "some people." But this much is true: Camping can be romantic. So if you've enjoyed camping experiences with your family, a romantic camping getaway is worth considering. Just you and your special someone, sitting by a crackling campfire underneath the starry skies. Another great time to connect.

It's not so romantic if insects give you the creeps, but you can create a unique experience by bringing wine and a meal to a campsite, rolling out a blanket and eating as the sun sets. Or you can eat at night with candlelight and the light of the moon. Many restaurants and grocery-store delis offer packaged meals for picnics that work perfectly.

Remember to bring along some music that you both enjoy. Your wedding song or something nostalgic would be perfect. Whatever works for you.

If you prefer to eat inside, away from the dirt and bugs, plan ahead and find a campsite near a restaurant where you want to have dinner. After that, you can head to the campsite to spend an evening together amid nature's splendor. You can hike, climb, ride bikes, rent a canoe, or do nothing but lounge around during your camping trip. The romantic part is having so much time to focus on one another. Quiet, uninterrupted, uncomplicated time together, and nothing is more romantic than that.

I don't know if that will make camping an aphrodisiac, but if it does, you don't have to thank me. You don't have to tell me, either. I don't need those kinds of details.

Simply Romantic

What is the number one romance killer?

No, it's not kids. It's stress. That's why I'm always leery of the elaborate romantic suggestions you'll find on the Internet. You know, something like this:

First, make a path of rose petals that leads from the door to the bedroom, then light no less than forty candles in the bedroom and have a bath waiting with a long-stemmed rose on one side and two glasses of champagne on the other, and then write a love poem and put it in a bottle and float it in the tub, and then. . . .

Fortunately, your plans don't have to be over-the-top to be romantic. You don't even have to leave your home.

"Romance is where you make it," said Melissa M. "You can have a romantic getaway in your own home if you make a conscious choice to do so."

Her suggestion was to get the chef of your favorite restaurant to assist in the preparation of a romantic meal or to have it catered. Buying some new linens and towels before the staycation might also give

Staycation Reward: Romantic Staycations

One romantic idea for couples is a hot air balloon ride or helicopter ride. Some balloon packages include champagne and dinner and allow a couple to ride alone (with the pilot). Helicopter rides are also thrilling, with the chance to fly over skyscrapers and get amazing views of a city.

To book a hot air balloon ride, visit *www.balloonridesacross america.com*. Be prepared to bring your wallet, however. These trips can cost almost $500 for a couple!

your home more of the "romantic hideaway" feel, she said. Sounds good to me: a romantic setting with no rose petals to clean up. I also like the idea of a candlelight dinner at home with food delivered.

Other simple romantic ideas include bike rides, day hikes, and renting rowboats. You can also take a picnic basket, and some wine or champagne, to a location with a view of the sunset. Playing a sport together or using your staycation to pursue a shared hobby such as photography or gardening is also a way to get quality time together.

Ready, Set, Stay

Author Elinor Glyn once said that "romance is the glamour which turns the dust of everyday life into a golden haze." What does that mean?

Well, I'm not sure. You probably need to ask a true romantic. Somebody who regularly carves "I love you" into a bar of soap or recites romantic poems on his lover's voicemail. But yes, we all want a little romance, so make it part of your staycation.

Just make it easy on yourself. Trying too hard almost defeats the purpose. So as you search for day trips and other activities to spend time together, think of the little ways you can make your staycation more romantic.

Tom M. found one of those ways in the aloe plants around his home. He said he gave his wife a "spa-quality aloe massage rub" that she loved. "Spa-quality" does sound impressive, doesn't it? My massages generally don't exceed "husband-quality."

If massages aren't your thing, try spending an evening watching your wedding video or other videos of your time together. Order food to be delivered, eat it by candlelight, and then write a letter or poem to your loved one and put it on his or her pillow. You can also plan "surprise days" in which one partner plans the day's events and picks out something the other

HOME IS WHERE THE WINE IS

Napa Valley in California is America's best-known area of wine production, but every state in the country has at least one winery. Yes, even Alaska, America's icebox. Yes, even Rhode Island, which is only slightly larger than this book.

At least one winery in every state, and in most cases, many more. So for wine lovers, it's a great staycation destination, but consider visiting a winery even if you're not a connoisseur of fine wine. You might like it even if you don't know if Pinot Grigio is a wine or Italy's best hope for an Olympic medal in gymnastics. Just remember that you have to get yourself back home, so have a designated driver or allow enough time to be safe after your last drink.

will love to do. Ice skating is even a romantic idea if you and your spouse already know how to skate a little. (Ice skating for the first time, however, is not such a good idea. It might be a better fit for the chapter on thrill rides.)

Keep it simple and you'll maximize the advantage of a staycation. But if you do have the time and energy to wow your loved one with rose petals, forty candles in the bedroom, champagne, and a love poem in a bottle floating in the bath, go for it. Just remember to use spell check on your poem. You can really ruin the moment by calling your sweetie "sweaty."

Help on the Net

- *www.4sitters.com*: Nationwide babysitter-finding service (membership required)
- *www.sittercity.com*: Nationwide babysitter-finding service (membership required)
- *www.seekingsitters.com*: Nationwide babysitter-finding service (membership required)
- *www.barefootstudent.com*: Listing of college students seeking babysitting work
- *www.bedandbreakfast.com*: Links to bed and breakfast locations, searchable by city
- *www.traintraveling.com*: Links to railroads with scenic day trips
- *www.lovingyou.com*: Huge list of romantic ideas, including ones submitted by readers
- *www.allamericanwineries.com*: List and contact information for U.S. wineries, organized by state

Quiz

Would camping in the backyard or at a museum or zoo be exciting for your kids?

Would your kids have fun making staycation postcards, designing a backyard steppingstone, or creating medals for a family Olympics?

Would a neighborhood scavenger hunt, a trip to a children's museum, or a train ride make your kids' staycation special?

Would your kids enjoy creating special holidays, theme days, or their own board game?

Do you want to put your kids in charge and let them plan some of the staycation?

If you answered "yes" to any of the above, you'll find ideas in "Especially for Kids" to make your staycation great for all ages.

Chapter 10
Especially for Kids

Children are the key to our future, but in the present, they're often seen as our baggage. I'm certainly guilty of feeling that way sometimes. I don't know how many times I've told my wife, "Well, we could've done that if we didn't have the kids."

But kids can make a staycation even better, and when we talk about kids and vacations, it's not so much the destination as getting there. If you embrace what's fun and exciting to them, they'll enjoy it much more, and so will you. That leads to a piece of advice before we get into the ideas for kids.

Never tell your kids that you're taking a staycation because you can't afford a traditional vacation. If your kids are teenagers, yeah, they'll figure it out. But there's no reason to emphasize it. And there's no reason to mention it at all to younger kids.

"I would for sure tell the kids that it's what we want to do, and that it's not because of money," said Joslyn T. "Once you act like it's a compromise, you won't have fun."

Instead, focus on all the fun things you'll be able to do together and tell them you'll have more time to spend together. That's important to the kids, especially young ones. My six-year-old and three-year-old ask me almost every morning, "Are you going to stay home all day today?"

Maybe that means I go to work too much. But I hope it means that what I do with my kids isn't as important as just doing something together. If you think that way about the time you spend with your kids during your staycation, it's probably going to be a success.

Before the staycation, have your kids make a list of the things they want to do. Discuss what you can fit into the time you have, give the kids options, and then make a plan. Maybe some of these will be part of it.

Theme Days

Kids, especially young kids, love gimmicks. That sounds bad, but what I mean is they like anything that has a special twist. You can do that with your staycation by having a theme for a day.

Or perhaps for a whole week. That's what Andy S., a dad with four kids, did during a staycation. It was a dinosaur theme, so Andy and his kids started with a trip to see fossils in a museum. The week also included a trip to Dinosaur Valley State Park in Glen Rose, Texas, where you can look at dinosaur tracks that are preserved in a riverbed and check out a pair of dinosaur statues: a 70-foot apatosaurus and a 45-foot tyrannosaurus rex. Finally, Andy and his kids went to a dried-out riverbed where fossils can be found.

Andy's kids loved it, and he pointed out to me that most cities have a place within driving distance to dig for fossils, gems, arrowheads, or other items kids will treasure. If your kids might like that, you can also set up a dinosaur dig in any sandbox or area with loose dirt. You can also buy pretend fossil kits at toy stores and online sites such as *www.discoverthis.com*. Kits include fossil models and excavating tools (chisel, brush, sponge, and so on). It's lots of fun for inquisitive kids.

The theme possibilities are countless, and they don't need to be complicated. Take volcanoes, for example.

You start by heading to the library for books on the subject. Then you make a volcano that erupts with vinegar and baking soda, and if your child is like my six-year-old, you make it erupt about a dozen times because it's still exciting every time. Then you finish the day by making a volcano cake or volcanic sundae (you can find recipes on the Internet) and watching a video on volcanoes from the library. You can also find video of volcano eruptions at sites such as *www.discovery.com*.

Another idea is a pirate day in which you make a pirate ship, decorate a treasure chest, and have each kid hide "treasure" and create a map for it. Or you can choose a silly theme, like a day devoted to the color green, with green eggs and ham for breakfast, green clothing, and making green ice cream. Another idea: Christmas in summer, with Christmas music, candy canes, making a Christmas tree, and watching a favorite holiday show. If it sounds silly to you, your kids will probably love it.

If you decide to have one theme for the vacation, let the kids decorate the house to fit the theme. Actually, even if there is no specific theme, it's not a bad idea to let the kids dazzle up the house with vacation decorations or craft projects. It will emphasize to them that this is a special time at home, not just the everyday.

Museum and Zoo Sleepovers

Do you remember sleeping over at a friend's house when you were a kid? Wasn't it a huge thrill?

These memories may consist of building a fort, staying up late, renting movies, battling your friends in video games, and playing outside. It was the ultimate fun experience.

Kids love sleepovers, so if they want to have a big slumber party during the week, a staycation might be a time for it. Or, if you want to keep the house a little more quiet, there are zoo and museum sleepovers that are gaining popularity.

A good example is at the Explora Museum in Albuquerque, New Mexico. The museum calls the overnight stay a "Camp-In" and tells kids and their parent chaperones to bring sleeping bags and pillows for an overnight stay. The campers get to spend the evening playing with the hands-on exhibits, seeing shows in the Explora Theater, and participating in fun experiments with staff members. Then they have a pizza dinner and sleep in the exhibit hall. That's how a science museum makes a visit special.

Art museums do the same thing. At sleepovers at the Art Museum of Greater Lafayette in Indiana, campers create paintings, work with clay, and then have a pizza dinner. After that, they are part of a scavenger hunt through the art gallery, and then watch a movie before bed. Check to see if your local art museum has a similar sleepover night. It's a great way to show kids that an art museum can be more than what they see during a school field trip.

Sleepovers are also popular at zoos. So popular, in fact, that some zoos offer several kinds: some for young kids with their parents, some for older kids,

HOW SWEET IS THE SUITE?

If you're planning a hotel stay with your kids, getting a suite is a great idea. But before you book a room, ask the hotel some questions about their suites. Some hotel suites only include a half wall between the sitting area and the sleeping area. This isn't a problem if you plan to go to bed at the same time as your kids, or if your kids can still fall asleep with the television on in the background. But if you have an infant or a toddler, it can be tricky. Fortunately, many hotel suites have pocket doors that close off the sleeping area from the sitting area. Ask a hotel manager about that, or if the hotel is near your house, ask to see one of the rooms.

some for families, and some limited to adults. The San Diego Zoo has a Safari Sleepover that includes a bus tour of the zoo, a campfire show, the chance to make s'mores, an evening zoo walk, a show with animals, and a guided moonlight walk to see nocturnal animals.

That's so much better than a typical zoo experience.

Trains, Trains, Trains

Nearly every kid, it seems, is fascinated by trains. If not fascinated, at least eager to ride on one. That was the case with the three-year-old twin daughters of Nancy Z. They didn't need to ride on a historic train or one that looked like Thomas the Tank Engine. A commuter train was fine.

"They have this whole mystery about the train," Nancy said. "Daddy has to go catch the train. Brenda [the nanny] has to go catch the train. So we took the mystery out of the train. We took it just two stops down, enough so they got a little taste of it."

At the end of the staycation, which also included trips to the park, touring around town like tourists, and backyard cookouts, it was the train ride that stood out to the kids. When they got home from the train ride, Nancy said, the kids made their own train with a big cardboard box. They're probably still asking their mom and dad to take them on the train again.

A commuter train might be a mundane experience for an adult, but for kids who don't get to ride it frequently, it's a thrill. It will be an even bigger thrill on a scenic train trip, which you can find at *www.traintraveling.com*. Kids will love any trip, whether it lasts for fifteen minutes or takes a few hours, but there are also special train rides designed for kids. Day Out with Thomas (find information at *www.thomasandfriends.com*) is a tour that gives kids a chance to ride in one of the coaches pulled by Thomas the Tank Engine. A similar tour allows kids to ride along with the Little Engine That Could, from the book by the same name. Tour information can be found at *www.thelittleenginethatcould.com*.

If you're planning a December staycation, many heritage railways also have Polar Express holiday train rides that include a visit with Santa. Search the Internet for "Polar Express" and your city to see if one is nearby.

Family Camp

Here's where you and your kids can be really creative. Whether you want to do it for one day or a whole week, you can create a summer camp at home.

Before the staycation begins, have the kids name the camp and decide what activities they want to be part of it. Then let them help schedule each day. You can include classic camp activities such as crafts, hiking, sports, bike rides, and singing, but it can be anything the kids want to do. As mentioned in the outdoors chapter, *www.horseandtravel.com* has links to stables that offer horseback riding.

Your home will be the camp headquarters, but you can leave each day for places such as local picnic spots, water parks, movie theaters, and museums. In the evening, you can do backyard s'mores using a grill or just roast marshmallows over a candle. A microwave s'more might seem crazy, but you can also do it that way. Just place a piece of chocolate bar on a graham cracker, top with a marshmallow, and microwave for about ten seconds. Your kids will like watching the marshmallow puff up as it melts.

It's camp, so including a sing-along makes sense. You can decide whether it's outside or inside, where neighbors can't hear your lovely singing voice. You can sleep in the comfort of your own bed, or as mentioned earlier, you can try camping in the backyard. Amy, Kevin, and their three kids love to do that.

"Living in a tent is by far our children's favorite," Amy said. "No need to go anywhere. Just pop the tent in the backyard and instant staycation."

Let the kids invite friends over to add to the fun. Also consider making camp T-shirts to wear during the staycation and keep as souvenirs. When I was a summer camp counselor at the YMCA, we made tie-dye T-shirts every year. The kids loved the shirts so much that we had to tell a few campers not to wear them everyday. It was turning into Camp Whatsthatsmell.

Backyard Olympics

A few years before I was a camp counselor, my friends and I staged our own neighborhood Olympics. We tried out several events, and it went pretty well until we attempted to pole vault in the front yard.

Do-it-yourself pole vault isn't a good idea, but your kids might like a family Olympics. The events can depend on the age of your kids, but it's better as a fun competition than a serious one. Long jump, Frisbee or ring toss, rope jumping, obstacle courses, and wheelbarrow and sack races are family-friendly events. You can even lay a two-by-four in the grass as a balance beam for the kids to do tricks on. Relay races are also a lot of fun, and if you can, have a piece of string at the finish line for the kids to break through. Actually, have lots of pieces of string so everyone gets a chance to feel the glory of breaking through the string at the finish line.

You can also have events at a community pool, a school track, or even a miniature golf course. The key is to have an event in which every child can be successful and to let kids help create the events. (If they suggest the javelin, however, give them a firm "No.")

> **YOU CAN TAKE IT WITH YOU**
> When driving to a staycation destination with your kids, you can make it more fun by taking along a fun treat that fits the theme. For a trip to the observatory or science museum, let the kids have moon rocks or freeze-dried ice cream, which are both available at *www .thespacestore.com*. On the way to hiking or camping, put together a kid's trail mix or make homemade cow pies by combining melted chocolate chips with raisins and almonds. Or, for any occasion, give in to a kid's fascination with gross stuff by melting butterscotch chips over chow mein noodles and peanuts to create "grasshopper guts."

As with the summer-camp idea, let your kids invite friends to be part of the Olympics. They'll all enjoy creating the medals, which can be made with construction paper or cardboard, wrapped with aluminum foil, and covered with glitter. You can also buy ribbons and make certificates for the winners. Certificates for kids, for any occasion, can be printed for free at *www.freeprintablecertificates.net*.

Making T-shirts is again a fun idea, and you can get easy iron-on letters for names on the back. There are also websites that allow you to design T-shirts online and then have them sent to you. Search the Internet for "custom T-shirts" and you'll find several to choose from including *www.customink.com*. That site provides lots of fonts for letters and clip art you can use to design the shirts, so the kids can be very creative. You can also make the shirts at any shop in your hometown that customizes clothing.

When the competition is over, don't forget the big finish. An awards presentation with the Olympic anthem playing, and maybe a pizza and ice cream buffet, is the perfect closing ceremony. Take pictures for the staycation scrapbook, and as with the real Olympics, administer random drug tests.

Okay, that last part is optional.

Letting Kids Take Charge

Kids should always have a say in the staycation activities, but sometimes it's fun to let them take control completely. It's certainly fun for them. Here are a few ideas:

Pint-sized Restaurant

We're not talking about fine dining, but this is a lot of fun for younger kids, especially if two or more of them are working together. Have the kids come up with a name for their restaurant and decide what will be served. (It doesn't have to involve cooking. It can just be peanut butter or turkey sandwiches.) Then have them create a menu, come up with prices, and select music to play at their restaurant. They might even want to provide live entertainment at their restaurant. It's all up to them.

Then you call the restaurant for reservations, get seated at a table, and the kids do the serving. You could be served a peanut butter and banana sandwich with pretzels as your meal, but the kids will like pretending to be adults. They might also offer you some very interesting desserts. You may end up deciding between milk with chocolate chips, marshmallows, and cereal in it or a hot dog bun spread with peanut butter and jelly.

Crazy Holidays

It's amazing how many silly holidays have been established. Hairstylist Appreciation Day, Wiggle Your Toes Day, National Chocolate Pudding Day . . . the list goes on and on. There's even National Take Your Dog to Work Day, which my employer has never embraced.

Anyway, have your kids get in on the fun by letting them come up with a holiday to celebrate each day. To get the ideas flowing, give them suggestions such as Eat Dessert First Day and Backward Hat Day. Then see what they come up with. You might end up being asked to wear a blue sock and a white sock for Crazy Socks Day or be part of Make Your Own Ice Cream Day. Encourage the kids to come up with special activities for each holiday, and if they want

STAYCATION POSTCARDS

Greetings from near home! That could be the message on the front of your staycation postcard, which kids will love to create. Take a photo of one of the staycation activities and attach it to cardstock paper and then have your child decorate around it. Or your child can decorate the entire postcard with pictures of fun times from the staycation. You can make it into a true postcard, or you might not want to mail them at all because the postcards make great souvenirs. The postcards can be tucked away in a scrapbook or put in a frame and hung in the living room. Well, maybe not the living room, but they're great for a kid's room.

Video Game Appreciation Day, that's okay, too. It's just one day, and maybe it can be your Get Some Peace and Quiet Day.

Kid Explorers

This one is simple. Take out a map, draw a circle with a 150-mile diameter (or other distance you find reasonable) around your house, and let your kids pick a town, or area of town, that they've never visited. Help them research what's in the towns around you at the library or on the Internet. If you only have one child, tell him or her to invite a friend.

When they decide on an attraction in a town, let them make a schedule of the day's events and even choose a place to eat lunch. You might not stick to the schedule, but the kids will enjoy setting the itinerary.

Back to Basics

There are lots of elaborate ways to make a staycation special for kids, but don't make things too complicated. This is your vacation, too, so it's supposed to be easy and relaxing. Josyln T. makes a good point when she says:

"We completely underestimate the power of simplicity with kids."

That's why part of Joslyn's staycation with her kids included filling up a kiddie pool with water and hanging out in the backyard. As they played, Joslyn and her husband got to relax with some grilled fajitas and margaritas. It was a nice night for the adults, too.

With young kids, keeping it simple really makes sense. We've all seen why, when a kid is more entertained by a big cardboard box than the toy it contained. And, in our staycation experiences, the simple things have made the biggest impact on my sons. Going bowling, a day at the water park, miniature golfing, a trip to a neighborhood playground . . . those were their highlights.

Nancy Z. kept it simple, too. Her staycation with her kids (three-year-old twins and an infant) included a kiddie pool in the backyard and going to the library to find books by children's author Sandra Boynton. They also spent an afternoon at the park with a friend.

"We slid, we swung," Nancy said. "Just a typical 'kids having fun not in their backyard' day."

The key phrase being "not in their backyard." You can keep a staycation simple without making it ordinary. You might even be able to keep it in your neighborhood the way staycationers Amy and Kevin did.

"We live in a great walking community adjacent to downtown Dayton, Ohio, and the pool, park, and tennis courts

STAYCATION STEPPINGSTONE
A family steppingstone is a fun and easy-to-make souvenir. Simple kits are available at stores such as Michael's, Hobby Lobby, or Joann Fabrics and Crafts and can also be ordered online. The kits come with the stone mix and colored pebbles to design the steppingstone, and you can write in the wet cement with a stick, just like every kid wants to do when he or she sees a patch of sidewalk drying. You might want to make a steppingstone and place it in your backyard to commemorate the staycation. Or, because the kits are so easy to use and can be found for as little as $15, you can get one for each family member and create a path. Remember to date the steppingstone, and years from now you'll have a great souvenir of your time together.

Staycation Reward: Especially for Kids

It won't be difficult to get younger kids excited about a staycation. They're thrilled to spend time with their parents. But adolescents know what kind of traditional vacations are out there. And they start knowing that Mom and Dad are like, totally not cool and not always right. They know it's a sacrifice. That's when a staycation is a tougher sell. In that case, your positive attitude is important. You have to show your kids that, although adolescent law requires that they shun you in public places, they can have fun on a staycation. And yes, throw in a little bribe.

Wait. Did I say "bribe"? I meant a reward. Your kids are part of the staycation, so they should be rewarded, too. Explain that with the money saved by taking a staycation, you'll be able to buy them that video game, mobile phone, or other electronic gadget they want. If your staycation is in the summer, you can also reward them with a shopping spree for school clothes.

The incentive can be something less expensive, such as buying movie tickets for your kids and their friends. Anything your kids can see as a tangible reward for saving money will help them understand the value of financial responsibility. You could also tell them that the staycation reward is being funneled to their college savings, but you probably won't get much response. Not a positive one, anyway. Perhaps a sigh and an eye roll.

are only three blocks away," Amy said. "There is really no reason for us to leave the neighborhood."

And that seems fine with their kids.

"Our kids were actually happier not to leave the state," Amy said. "We have lugged them along for so long and they hate traveling in a car for more than three hours. As a matter of fact, the two girls have become carsick within the last three years. They prefer to stay home, so the idea of a staycation was good for them."

Ready, Set, Stay

Wax museums, Guinness World Records Museums, and Ripley's Believe It or Not Museums are great for kids of any age. So are family amusement centers (discussed in the "Theme Parks and Thrill Rides" chapter), skating rinks, and city recreation centers. Scavenger hunts, in your home or the neighborhood, are also fun. You can also buy a croquet, badminton, or volleyball set for your backyard or turn on the hose and roll out a Slip 'N Slide. Younger kids will like making a puppet theater out of a large box and putting on a show, and older kids might like making a movie during their staycation.

Another idea is to have your kids make their own board game. You can order "Make Your Own Opoly" on the Internet, which is a kit for creating a personalized version of Monopoly (or a game much like it). The game comes with software that allows you to use your own photos and design the game board on a computer. After the design is complete, it's printed out on stickers that attach to a blank game board.

Or your kids, and you, can create a totally new game. All you need is a game board, which can be found at a thrift store, garage sale, or in the box of a game you never play anymore. Cover the board with computer sticker paper or contact paper, leaving a small uncovered sliver so the board can fold. Then design the game on it with markers. It's a good idea to write down your plans for the game before starting to mark on the board, but extra stickers and contact paper are good for "do overs."

More Ideas

A "Cookie Day" is exciting for kids. Roll out some sugar cookie dough and let the kids make cookies in their favorite shapes (or just circles if you don't have cookie cutters). Bake the cookies, let them cool, and then let the kids decorate them. Spread vanilla frosting on top; then they can add chocolate chips, raisins, nuts, M&Ms, candy sprinkles, and anything else they want on the cookies. Make the cookies at the start of the staycation and the kids will have a fun treat for the days that follow. If your staycation falls during the Christmas season, kids will love building a gingerbread house with graham crackers. They love eating it even more, which is why my three-year-old's last gingerbread house had some serious structural problems.

A "Fun with Science" Day is also an idea. Experiments with paper airplanes, balancing eggs, and the classic bubbling mixture of baking soda and vinegar are easy and fun. For older kids, the science day can include electricity kits that allow them to connect circuits to make fans, lights, and sirens work. You can find those at toy stores or online. You can also find dozens of ideas for home science experiments at *www.bizarrelabs.com*.

Having a day devoted to art is also fun for kids. You'll find lots of ideas for crafts at *www.family-crafts.about.com*, and hobby and craft stores have kits for painting, sewing, stamping, engraving, clay modeling, weaving baskets, and even pottery. Maybe the day will ignite your child's passion for art, and twenty years from now, she will paint a masterpiece that will hang in an art gallery you can visit on another staycation. Or maybe her art will be shown during a commercial that screams, "Starving Artists Sale! Everything Must Go! Rock-Bottom Prices!"

Well, that's a problem for another day. But for now, there are many, many ideas. There is also one essential ingredient that makes all those ideas work: Your attitude.

HOME IS WHERE THE MEMORY IS

When I was a kid, my dad would pull out the 8 millimeter family filmstrips, put them on the reel, and aim the projector at a living-room wall. Family videos have come a long way since then, but it's still a great bonding time for a family, and you can make it special by treating it like a movie. Pop popcorn, buy candy at the store, and have any other treats that you typically take to the theater. If you have a video camera, hopefully you will videotape some of the time spent on your staycation. Consider reserving the last night of the staycation as a movie night featuring some of that video. You can relive some of your staycation before watching other home videos or a rented movie.

Keeping Your Staycation Positive

"It's important to have the right attitude about taking a staycation, especially when children are included, so everyone knows in advance what fun activities everyone will be enjoying and there's no worries and whining about being bored," Lin B. said. "Getting the entire family involved in the planning of activities is key when children are involved and putting in the effort to show the kids that there will be lots of fun things going on."

There will be lots of fun things going on. But you have to create the fun tone for your kids. You have to make sure the staycation feels like an alternative to a vacation, not a sacrifice. You have to make them buy into it.

Come on, now. Isn't that putting a lot of weight on my shoulders? That seems like a lot of responsibility for a time that's supposed to be relaxing and carefree.

Well, my friend, you decided to have kids. Aren't they a blessing?

Actually, even with sarcasm removed, kids really are a blessing. And making a staycation special for your kids isn't difficult. It can be as simple as breaking the rules to let them stay up later and making the kind of meals they'll only get during a staycation.

Nancy Z. did that for her kids during their staycation, including one dinner with macaroni and cheese and milkshakes.

"We're not the healthiest family anyway, but it was definitely a time of, if you want that, that's okay," Nancy said. "You want pasta for breakfast? I'm okay with that. Very laid back."

That's the right attitude. If you're having fun, your kids will know it. If you're upbeat about the staycation, they will be, too. That was the experience for Melissa M., who said she took her kids to tours of places such as ice cream and cheese factories and let them snack on the samples for lunch.

"Then we'd stop at the A&W Drive-In in Vermont, the last one in the region, for a float," Melissa said. "It was cheap, but an adventure, and they loved it. They still talk about it like it was a four-course gourmet meal."

Yes, it's up to you to make it special. But that's not a burden, it's an opportunity. You can be a kid again.

Isn't that one of the great things about being a parent?

Help on the Net

- *www.discoverthis.com*: Site that sells educational toys, including a fossil-dig kit
- *www.traintraveling.com*: Links to railroads with scenic day trips
- *www.thomasandfriends.com*: Schedule and information for Day Out with Thomas train rides
- *www.thelittleenginethatcould.com*: Schedule and information for Little Engine That Could train rides
- *www.freeprintablecertificates.net*: Printable award certificates for a variety of occasions
- *www.customink.com*: Site for designing and ordering custom T-shirts
- *www.familycrafts.about.com*: Ideas and instructions for crafts for kids
- *www.familyfun.com*: Ideas for family-friendly activities
- *www.bizarrelabs.com*: Instructions for easy science experiments with kids
- *www.ripleys.com*: Links to Ripley's Believe It or Not museums

Chapter 11
Some More Ways to Pack in Fun

Welcome to the chapter for the ideas that didn't fit anywhere else. It's kind of like the "potpourri" category on the game show *Jeopardy!* but with no questions about the topography of Liechtenstein or the four U.S. presidents in three different centuries who were born in the same county.

Before we get to some more ideas, however, let's discuss the final staycation rule. You'll like this one: There are no rules. Yes, I know I've given you a whole bunch of rules and now I'm saying there are no rules. So I'll clarify: sThere are no rules that cannot be broken. A staycation can be whatever you want it to be. You can schedule your days tightly or allow for a leisurely pace. You're not at the mercy of flight schedules or hotel checkout policies. You can take an idea and go with it.

"You have to be able to see what's right in front of you, and for most of us, that's not an easy task," said Melissa M. "The grass is always greener in Jamaica or Orlando or Europe. Or is it?"

Sure it is. Even with all the hassles of travel, the big, splashy getaway will always be the dream vacation. But if you don't have deep pockets, a deep well of creativity will take you a long way.

That served Cristi C. well during one of her staycation days in Dallas. She and a friend had lunch at a trendy, but casual, restaurant and then headed over to a bar at an upscale hotel.

"We sat at the pool bar, people-watching the regulars from the Dallas area who were mingling in the pool as we drank mojitos and met visitors from all over the country," Cristi said. "We had a great time, and it felt like an oasis getaway even though I was less than five minutes from home."

Less than five minutes from home. That's really maximizing the area where you live. Now let's talk about some other ways to do it.

Block Parties

A great way to fill a day with fun is a neighborhood party. Police departments encourage the parties because they help neighbors get to know each other, and tighter-knit neighborhoods are safer. The parties also are a way to get people interested in a Neighborhood Watch Program, and another plus is that you might find a neighbor who is a qualified contractor, electrician, mechanic, or—yes!—a babysitter who doesn't mind working on Saturday nights.

But forget about those benefits. A block party is just fun, which makes it perfect for scheduling into your staycation. Planning ahead is the most important thing. At least a month before the party, pick a weekend to have the party and then pass out invitations to neighbors. Potlucks are best, especially if it's the first block party in your neighborhood, and you can provide drinks or tell people to bring them. Have people RSVP so you'll know how many people to expect. You'll probably find someone willing to help organize the party with you.

STAYCATION BONUS #4:
NO SUITCASE TO UNPACK

You return from a long road trip or plane flight, lie down on the bed, and then you see it: the suitcase you need to unpack. It's not the biggest chore ever, but unpacking the suitcase is a real downer. Packing isn't fun, either, but at least you have the vacation ahead of you. Unpacking the suitcase is like taking down Christmas lights. The fun's over. It's just an annoying task.

It doesn't need to be complicated. A nearby park can be the site, or someone's driveway or front lawn, or a cul-de-sac if the homeowners don't mind. If you have a lot of kids in the neighborhood, you can ask neighbors if they want to chip in to rent a bounce house. And if you plan far enough in advance, you can probably also get local firefighters to drive the truck over for kids to look at and/or a police officer who will stop by, hand out sticker badges, and put the lights and siren on for the kids. Other inexpensive ways to keep the kids interested include bubbles, Frisbees, sidewalk chalk, water balloons, and glow sticks.

If you want to add more frills to the party, search "block party ideas" on the Internet and you'll find advice from people who have put them together. A couple notes of warning, however. If you live in a community with a homeowners' association, there might be special rules you must follow. And large parties that require blocking off part of a residential street usually need a special-event permit.

Starting a New Hobby

For Christmas, my three-year-old got a guitar from his grandparents. Not a full-size guitar, but one big enough that he can strum it, sing Wiggles songs, and accidentally bang it into his bedroom wall. When he's a few years older, we're going to take guitar lessons together.

Maybe we'll take the lessons during a staycation, because that's a great time to start learning an instrument. A staycation gives you the time to take professional lessons, practice, and decide whether you want to continue. Links to instructors for instruments, as well as voice lessons, can be found for your hometown at *www .privatelessons.com*. Group music lessons are also offered through city recreation departments and as continuing education courses at community colleges. Music stores—the ones that sell instruments, not CDs—also have bulletin boards with music teachers seeking students.

Other popular hobbies include photography, sewing, pottery-making, and painting, and you can find classes and clubs to get you started in any of them. My wife's mom, who passed away years ago, was into miniature collecting and made intricate scenes inside wooden boxes. We still have some, and they're amazing. It turns out a lot of people are into miniatures, and there is a National Association of Miniature Enthusiasts. At the association's website, *www.miniatures.org*, you can find links to local miniatures clubs.

Another easy hobby to get into is video editing. Camcorders are all digital now, so any video you shoot can be edited on a computer. It allows you to cut out the boring, jiggly, hard-to-watch stretches of video, leaving you with a shorter video

STAYCATION VOLUNTEERING
During Brenda and Ed's last staycation, their oldest daughter came up with an idea: Why not do something to help the community? So the family volunteered for Habitat for Humanity, a nonprofit organization that builds affordable housing for low-income households. Ed, Brenda, and their three kids spent a day working on the house and then committed to spend one day per month volunteering for the organization. Volunteering makes you feel great, and if you have kids, they'll feel proud to help. And as they pick up trash at the park, read books to kids at a community center, help at the food bank, or visit a homeless shelter, they'll learn the importance of sacrifice. They'll know that one person can make a difference. Finding a way to volunteer is easy with *www.volunteermatch.org*. Just type in your zip code and you'll find ways to volunteer in your area.

you'll actually have time to watch. Even better, editing allows you to add text to your videos, graphics, special effects, narration, and music. You can feel like you're making a movie, or at least a music video.

It's also cheap and easy. Personal computers come loaded with Windows Movie Maker, and if you're a Mac user, you've got iMovie on your computer. It's easy to learn, and the results are very rewarding. If you shoot an hour's worth of staycation footage, you can save all the raw video and also create a five- or ten-minute montage of the best moments. Add in some still photos and some background music—"Our House" by Crosby, Stills, Nash and Young, perhaps—and you'll have a great memento of your staycation. It can also be e-mailed out to friends or posted on a video-sharing site such as YouTube.

Once you realize what you can do with video, and you must feed the addiction, you can find books on video editing at the library and also clubs and online forums for editing enthusiasts. You can find lots of advice at *www.videomaker.com*.

Virtual Vacation

Virtual worlds are becoming more and more popular on the Internet. Websites such as *www.secondlife.com*, *www.thesimsonline .com*, and *www.cybertown.com* allow you to customize an avatar (an online identity) and interact with others in a "massively multiplayer online role-playing game." If that sounds weird to you, you're not alone. The sites actually allow you to shop, with real money, for virtual items.

Staycation Reward: You Make the Call

This book is written for budgets of all sizes, so the staycation reward will be defined differently by each person. My preference right now is to take most of the staycation reward and sock it away in savings because I know it's just a matter of time before one of my kids falls off the monkey bars, takes a spill on a bike, or runs into a car while playing street football. They've got my genes. It's going to happen.

Or maybe one of them will be a music protégé who needs private lessons to fulfill his talent. Or a young swimming star who, with the right coach and training, could be an Olympic gold medalist. Or . . .

Well, it's never a problem to save too much money. That's probably why you have taken, or are planning to take, a staycation. But you have to be able to splurge a little. Even if it's just one night out for dinner, a movie you've wanted to see, or a pair of shoes that are calling out to you, find a small way to reward yourself. Try to break the rules a little. It helps a staycation feel like a vacation.

For those of us not interested in spending real money on things that don't exist in real life, you may want to consider the alternative virtual vacation. You can create a trip overseas by immersing yourself in a different culture through cuisine, language lessons, and films.

The *Wall Street Journal* ran a story about a woman in New York who did that. She viewed Japanese films, shopped at traditional Japanese markets, and bought souvenirs there. She ordered in Japanese at the restaurant and partook in traditional Japanese activities.

If there's a country or area of the United States that you want to visit or know more about, you can take a virtual vacation there. With a library and the Internet, it's easier than ever to find information about customs, clothing, food, films, music, and the history of an area.

You can also take advantage of Google Earth (*www.earth.google .com*), a free Internet application that provides satellite images, maps, terrain, and 3-D views of buildings from all over the world. A few years ago a global poll decided the new "Seven Wonders of the World." With Google Earth and other websites on the Internet, you can virtually visit the Great Wall of China, the Colosseum in Rome, the Taj Mahal in India, and the other new wonders of the world.

Google Earth also lets you look at stars and galaxies. It's a great educational tool for you and your kids, and can be combined with a trip to an observatory or stargazing during a camping trip. And although I don't own Google stock and I'm still waiting for an "I've been Googled" T-shirt to be sent to me, here's another free Google treat to check out: Google maps (*www.maps.google.com*).

The maps offer street-level pictures for areas all over the United States, as well as in several other countries. Google sends out teams of people with cameras mounted on dashboards to take photos all over the country, and the result is a massive collection of photos of downtown areas, tourist spots, and residential areas that you can find on a map. It's fun to look at different areas of the country, especially if you've lived in several states and want to see your old stomping grounds. It's addicting, but even if you waste time, you won't waste money. Virtual jeans and shoes are not for sale.

The website *www.earthcam.com* is also a way to virtually travel the world. It has links to webcams all over, so you can watch people on the Las Vegas strip, check out a beach somewhere, or get a live view of thousands of other places. There are even links to several water park webcams. Nothing spectacular, but a fun taste of what's going on in the world.

Planning Your Next Vacation

So what are your plans for your next big vacation? A trip to Europe? An Alaskan cruise? Sitting on the beach in Cabo San Lucas, Mexico?

If you're like me, someday you'll take your kids to Disney World (or your wife to Cabo San Lucas) and go all out. You can go for a week, stay in a resort hotel, and make it really special. However, if you're like me, you're just not sure when that someday will be. Other expenses take priority right now.

But you can still start planning your next vacation. Not actually booking hotel rooms, of course, but just researching the possibilities.

Check out flights, resorts and hotels, tourist sites, and other attractions. Find out where you want to go and what you want to do when the time is again right for a traditional vacation. It's a good way to stay positive and look toward the future, and that money you save by taking a staycation can kickstart your saving for the big vacation.

You can even use part of your staycation to raise money for the big vacation. Classic fundraisers include mowing lawns, babysitting, walking dogs, and car washes, and a garage sale can be a fun family project if everyone gets involved in deciding what to sell, designing signs, and making price tags. Or you can be more creative by starting a family business for a day or two. I know a family who created a "pet photography day" in their neighborhood, and they made it a success by posting fliers a few days beforehand so friends and neighbors could plan to be there. It turned into a small-scale block party, but the family also made some money by charging two dollars per picture.

Home-Exchange Vacations

It's the vacation at somebody else's house, which doesn't exactly fit the definition of a staycation. But it's creative, saves money, and many people don't consider it.

The idea behind a home-exchange vacation is for two people, couples, or families to swap houses during their vacation. For example, your family could swap houses with a family at the other end of the street to give you a completely different view of the neighborhood.

Just kidding. Unless you really, really want to get out of your house, the families in a home exchange would be in different parts of the country or world. The obvious benefit is saving a lot of money on a hotel, but home swappers also can save on some restaurant meals by dining in and car rental if car use is part of the swap. The added bonus, especially if you're staying in a foreign country, is getting a more authentic experience of the area than staying in a hotel.

The idea has become popular enough that there are several websites with listings of people who want to swap homes. If you pay a membership fee (usually less than $100), you can create a listing for your home and see others at *www.homelink.org*, *www.intervacus.com*, and *www. homeexchange.com*. The listings include dates that homes are available, square footage, distance to popular destinations, and other amenities. There are contractual issues to sort out with a swap, you'll still have to pay to drive or fly to the home where you'll be staying, and the thought of strangers alone in your home might give you the willies.

LET'S TALK ABOUT FOOD
Food is a staple of the vacation experience, and you undoubtedly have a favorite local restaurant. That favorite restaurant has a place in your staycation, but to create the vacation environment, why not try something new? Consider this staycation tip from Joslyn T.: "It's about pushing yourself to do something you wouldn't normally do. It's about forcing yourself out of your comfort zone."

However, the idea is still worth considering. A staycation is a way to maximize the vacation you can afford, and a home exchange can help you do that. If you do a home swap with someone who is within a day's drive, you won't need to rent a car and you'll save enough on hotel costs to offset travel expenses. Then you can explore a different city than your own while getting the financial benefits of a staycation.

One way to break your staycation out of the ordinary is to spend a week sampling international foods. Visit a Thai restaurant one night, a Mexican eatery the next, and finish with Italian, French, or German food. You can get recommendations on all types of food from sites such as *www.roadfood.com* and *www.chowhound.com*, which have user reviews of restaurants across the country. If you like to cook or bake, try experimenting with something new. If it doesn't work out, you can just laugh it off and head to a restaurant.

More Possibilities

Now we really get into it. Five quick ideas that have little in common other than fitting into staycation plans. It's the *Jeopardy!* potpourri category, so we'll play it like the game show, with the answer in the form of a question.

100 points

These free- or low-cost events include lots of horsepower, are great for adults and kids, and are entertaining even for those who think a V-8 only refers to vegetable juice.

What are new and classic car shows?
Admission is rarely more than a few dollars, and even if the show includes an auction, browsers always outnumber the buyers.

You can find the shows advertised in the automotive section of your local newspaper and a schedule for shows across the nation at *www.carshownews.com*.

200 points

If you can't get to Vegas but still want a little bit of casino excitement, these might interest you.

What are the casinos that are located in more than half the states?
They range from large casinos such as Mohegan Sun in Connecticut and the Trump Taj Mahal in New Jersey to smaller casinos such as Harrah's Council Bluffs in Iowa and Spirit Mountain in Oregon. You can find hundreds more by searching "list of U.S. casinos" on *www.wikipedia.org*.

300 points

You'll probably never be able to afford a dream house, but this is very affordable.

What is a luxury home tour?
These tours, often done as fundraisers for charities, allow you to tour high-end homes before they are sold. The best way to find them is by calling a local realty agency, but they are also promoted in local style and home-décor magazines, and you'll find more by searching for "luxury home tours" on the Internet.

400 points

This is an idea that, because it again involves beer, will lead you to think I'm too into malted beverages.

What is sampling the products at a local microbrewery?
Unlike the large brewery tours, you're almost certain to find a microbrewery near you. Search the database at *www.beermapping .com* and you'll find places such as the Anderson Valley Brewing Company in Boonville, California, which has a restaurant and daily tours of its brewing area.

500 points

This classic hobby has no "wow" factor, but it's a simple pleasure that often gets squeezed out of our busy lives.

What is reading a good book?
Oh yeah, and it's free. Just head to the library. If you have kids, you can even use the daily theme idea from the last chapter. Read a book and create an activity based on that book, such as cooking a meal that fits its setting, or create a trivia game or board game based on the book.

Ready, Set, Stay

When I told a friend that I was writing a book about staycations, she asked what would be in it. "It will have inspiration and encouragement," I told her. That's what I hoped would be in the book, but what I knew would be in the book were lots of ideas for filling a staycation.

"You mean like playing board games at home?" she said.

Uh . . . not really. I've played so many games of Candy Land, Chutes and Ladders, and Hungry, Hungry Hippos with my kids that it's nearly as boring as the lectures by my college geography professor, Mr. Nytol. I'm thrilled that my oldest son has advanced to the slightly more intellectually stimulating UNO card game.

But of course board games can be part of a staycation. If you want to order some pizza and have a family game night, that's easy and inexpensive. Or if you want to have an adult game party (and yes, I know that sounds x-rated, but this is good, clean fun), you can have people over for dinner and cocktails and play any of the hundreds of games on the market.

As Carrie S. said:

HOME IS WHERE THE CREATIVITY IS

"Money is always an issue in our family," Carrie S. said, "so extravagant vacations are few and far between." For staycations, Carrie replaces extravagance with creativity. During a recent stay at a nearby hotel, she spent a Saturday swimming and lounging by the pool. She then found out the hotel's ballroom was the site of a high school prom. "So on Saturday night, we changed into our PJs and sat at the lobby lounge and watched the parade," she said. The promgoers probably thought it was hilarious, but Carrie and her family had a great time. The following day, the family fueled up with the hotel's Sunday brunch buffet and spent a few hours at a local festival before driving home. "Sometimes you just need a change from the everyday," Carrie said, "and we try to look for little ways to enliven our routine."

"A staycation is about being together as a family, or a couple, or whatever you are."

So if a board game fosters togetherness, go to it. It's just that playing board games sounds pretty mundane, and it's probably what many people think of when they hear about the concept of a staycation.

You know by now that a staycation can be much more than that. Hopefully the ideas in this book will help make that happen, but you know your hometown better than me. You also know your budget, your spouse and family, and your favorite activities.

We're all different. Some of us want tickets to the ballet; some of us want tickets to the baseball game. Some want a quiet hike on a mountain trail; some want to fly down the trail on a mountain bike. Some consider opera a beautiful combination of story, music, and the power of the human voice; some see it as a show that moves too slowly, has people singing much too loudly, and needs more chase sequences.

Yes, we're all different. But whether we're strapped for cash or just tired of being strapped into an airline seat, we want the same thing from our staycation. So let's throw it back to Alex Trebek for Final *Jeopardy!*

Answer: Although staycationers are as varied as New England clam chowder and Texas barbecue, this is what every staycationer wants.

Question: What is a stay-at-home vacation that really feels like a vacation?

Congratulations, you've qualified for the next chapter. You might have won some fabulous parting gifts as well, but I'll have to check on that.

Help on the Net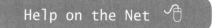

- *www.privatelessons.com*: List of music instructors, searchable by area and specialty
- *www.miniatures.org*: Home of National Association of Miniature Enthusiasts
- *www.videomaker.com*: Instructions for editing home videos
- *www.volunteermatch.org*: Helps people find volunteer opportunities close to home
- *www.earth.google.com*: Home of Google Earth, a free service with satellite images of the world
- *www.maps.google.com*: Home of Google Maps, a free service that includes street views of many areas
- *www.earthcam.com*: Links to webcams around the world
- *www.homelink.org, www.intervacus.com, www.homeexchange.com*: Membership sites with listings for vacation home exchanges
- *www.roadfood.com, www.chowhound.com*: Reviews of restaurants around the country
- *www.carshownews.com*: Schedules of classic car shows in the United States
- *www.beermapping.com*: Maps and links to microbreweries in the United States

Chapter 12
Making the Most of It

As I was researching this book, I found the website *www.needa vacation.com*. I also found *www.ineedavacation.com* and *www.uneed avacation.com*. And if I need a vacation and "u" need a vacation, well then doesn't it make sense that there's a "weneedavacation.com"?

Yes, we all need a vacation. Studies have even shown the health benefits.

But do those benefits only come from a big, traditional vacation that takes you to another part of the country or world? Do you need to hop on a plane or take a long road trip to get good mileage from your vacation time?

Depends on your perspective. First, here are four qualities of a good vacation:

1. *Relaxing*

A vacation needs to be a stress-buster. Far away or near home, it has to let you break free from the hectic pace of your everyday life.

2. *Responsibly budgeted*

If you can't afford the vacation, it won't be relaxing. Squishing your toes in the white sands of a beach in Hawaii will only put you at ease until the bill comes due. And the views of the turquoise waters in the Bahamas are no more breathtaking than the credit card statement that follows. What's the point of trying to relieve stress by adding more stress?

3. *Flexible*

Your life is one big calendar, and you fill in a square each day. You're on a schedule and facing a deadline. So although you must plan ahead for a vacation, you need the freedom to change gears at any time. Slow down, speed up . . . whatever makes each day feel right.

4. *Satisfying*

I hope you've taken a vacation that was fantastic. The kind of vacation in which you completely forgot about your assignments at work, the clanking noise in the car, and the neighbor who practices drumming at 2 A.M. That is a truly satisfying vacation—one that leaves you with lasting memories and feeling recharged.

Now let's look at how a staycation stacks up.

Can a Staycation Be Relaxing?

Well, it certainly should be. After all, you'll be in control of the itinerary instead of an airline that is rarely on time. You won't worry about what luggage you need to check and whether it will make it to your destination with you. There will be no waiting in lines at the airport, no questions such as "Have you had control of your bag since you packed it?", and no chance you'll be randomly selected for a baggage inspection or body search.

Another plus is that you won't have to talk to anyone on a plane. Many of us are social people and welcome exchanging small, day-to-day pleasantries with strangers. But on an airplane, many of us prefer to put on some headphones, read a book, or browse through *SkyMall* magazine for bizarre products such as three-foot garden gnomes and the world's greatest nose-hair trimmer.

Airplane conversation is bad because it's hard to hear when you're in the air, and once the conversation begins, there's a good chance it won't end until you land. Talking creates an expectation of more talking, and trying to end the conversation is sometimes awkward. That's why on one two-hour flight, I learned how the passenger next to me felt about flu shots, her kids' academic progress, her view of the newspaper industry, and her husband's French-Canadian heritage. I also learned some French phrases, but none of them were, "Thank you, but I'd like to take a nap now."

Vacationing is fun, no doubt about it. But there's a reason that a travel company named itself "Worry-Free Vacations." Vacations, or at least ones that involve traveling, are filled with worry.

A staycation will also allow you to sleep in your own bed most nights. That means you won't have to worry about the hit-or-miss quality of hotel beds, and you'll have your own pillow. Maybe I'm a pillow snob, but even at nice hotels, I have a hard time finding a pillow that isn't either too fluffy or so flat it almost folds like a towel. That's why after more than a couple of nights away from home, I'm usually sleep-deprived.

Lin Yutang, a Chinese writer and philosopher, put it this way:

"No one realizes how beautiful it is to travel until he comes home and rests his head on his old, familiar pillow."

So, so true.

The Vacation Destination

One thing no one can deny is that in most cases, a destination vacation provides a lot of time for relaxation once you get there. And honestly, your home can't compare. The traditional vacation clearly has the staycation beat in creating the vacation environment. So what's important for staycationers is to maximize what they've got.

"The key is to have all the chores done, no projects scheduled, and a willingness to avoid them," Tom M. said.

Exactly. Because just knowing you don't have to do anything is relaxing.

Is a Staycation Responsibly Budgeted?

Vacations often aren't.

Everyone wants to have a nice vacation, but funding it with credit cards or by spending the money you need to pay bills is a huge mistake.

You'll have no such problem with a staycation, even if you splurge on some things. Not only will you save on travel costs and overpriced hotel rooms, but there won't be the unexpected costs of a vacation.

And there are always unexpected costs. According to a study by professional services firm PricewaterhouseCoopers, the U.S. hotel industry made $1.75 billion in fees in 2007. Fees for things such as bottled water, towels, telephone use, and—my favorite—parking. You may pay $15 a night just for the privilege of parking your car at the hotel where you're staying.

Another sign that hotels are nearly as desperate as airlines to shake cash out of you is the "energy fee." Some hotels add that to the bill, even though they have no idea how much energy you used in your room. And remember the courtesy of a hotel holding a bag for you for a few hours before you checked in or checked out? That seems to be coming to an end. Most hotels now charge a few bucks to hold your bag. It's a courtesy fee, but there is nothing courteous about it. Can I charge the hotel three bucks for my courtesy in returning the room key?

A staycation saves you on the heavy taxes tacked on to a hotel room, and you'll also save on ridiculous rental-car taxes. The National Business Travel Association has spoken out against the explosion of rental taxes in recent years, and there's good reason why. If you rent a car for $40 a day, you'll probably pay another $20 in federal, state, county, and local taxes; airport surcharges; transportation fees; and facility usage charges. You might even help pay for a new sports arena or performance hall. That's nice of you.

Think of all the tax money your staycation will save. It gives you another reason to splurge. (But sorry high-def fans, it's still not enough for the 50-inch plasma or LCD TV.)

Is a Staycation Flexible?

Yes, even with all the rules listed in the early chapters, a staycation is very flexible. You can pack one day full of activities and take the next day at a more leisurely pace. You can even squeeze in some time to run a couple of errands and take care of a household project.

I know, I know, I forbade you to take care of such projects during your staycation. But I was probably a little hasty in saying you should never let a household project invade your vacation environment. Several of the staycationers I talked to mentioned that as a big positive of their staycation experience. The important part, however, was that each staycationer kept the vacation mindset.

"We enjoyed the freedom of being home and having the ability to cross items off the to-do list without being overwhelmed and pressed for time," Katie H. said. "I really liked that we limited our to-do list to one item per day. That way we knew that one item had to be taken care of, but it wasn't lingering over our heads reminding us at every turn."

"It's important to balance your staycation between resting, not doing anything that requires effort, doing fun things around town, and catching up on errands and house stuff," said Brian W. "By balancing those things, a vacation isn't boring, but fun and productive."

Some of you may still cringe at the idea of being productive on a staycation. But it's your vacation, so do what works best for you. With a staycation, you have that flexibility.

Is a Staycation Satisfying?

Now we've reached the sticking point for many people considering a staycation. If they take a trip to a popular vacation site such as Hawaii, New York City, or Disney World, they know they'll be entertained. They know they'll come back with lasting memories, stories to tell, and pictures to show friends.

But a staycation? Well, it's a big wildcard. Lots of people are taking staycations, and even more are talking about them, but the idea seems so mundane. It's like comparing watching a football game or concert on television with the experience of actually being there. It's not a real vacation. It's a fake-cation, even without the requirement of a high-pressure sales pitch about timeshares.

No, a staycation is not a fake-cation. But the analogy of watching a big event versus being there in person isn't off the mark. A staycation is never going to match the trip to Australia or the Caribbean cruise, but how you treat the staycation is what makes the difference. It's what you do to make the ordinary at least a little bit extraordinary.

Here was the staycation week for Katie and Chris, as told by Katie:

"We visited a local sake company for a tour and tasting, went to the local zoo, visited a local state park that we've been meaning to visit forever, walked down to our local ice-cream shop, went to the gym five days a week, got enough sleep, hooked up our furloughed ice maker, fixed a broken sprinkler, visited with friends, sun dried tomatoes in our backyard, and went to the batting cages.

For some people, that would never work. But for Katie and Chris, "It was an unequivocal success," Katie said.

Staycationing was also a success for Melissa M., who has made visiting local restaurants a focus of her plans. She also likes visiting Shaker communities near her home in Massachusetts, finding country fairs and craft shows, and touring different museums, including a beer-can museum.

The hardest part, Melissa said, was getting her husband to eat at local restaurants but spend the way he would on a vacation.

"He kept wanting to cheap out," she said.

That's easy to do, and it's not always bad. As long as you don't feel constrained by a budget all the time, or controlled by the things you have to do. That's what helped Nancy Z. have a successful staycation with her husband and kids. She didn't worry about daily chores, and she let her kids have later bedtimes and eat the foods they liked best. Nancy also put together fun day trips and enjoyed backyard barbecues.

Simple stuff, but by the end of the staycation, she saw the advantages.

"After I go on vacation, I always feel I need a vacation from my vacation," Nancy said. "You come back so tired. This was just so relaxing and awesome, and I would highly recommend it to anyone."

So would I. A staycation might not match the dazzle of a traditional vacation, but it can be just as much fun. My last vacation was a family staycation that included trips to water parks, amusement centers, movies, the science and nature museums, the library, and a baseball game. There also was a bowling extravaganza with my six-year-old, who likes to throw heavy objects. I'd rather he does that at a bowling alley than in our living room.

We didn't take a flight, we didn't rent a car, and we didn't travel farther than fifty miles out of town. But we did have a great time on our staycation. It was relaxing, it fit our budget, and it was flexible enough to work around two of my kids getting sick for a day. That would've been a nightmare on a traditional vacation.

The staycation really was satisfying. And when it was over, I didn't feel like I had sacrificed anything.

Living It Up, Staycation Style

Still, it's hard not to get jealous when you hear about friends' grandiose vacation plans. So I guess that's an acknowledgment that a staycation is a sacrifice. But anyone who takes a staycation and focuses on how it's a sacrifice will no doubt be disappointed. That's why I wrote in the introduction: "A staycation is most successful when you have a positive attitude and willingness to adjust the traditional notion of what a vacation is."

You live in the now, but plan for the future. You make responsible choices. When life gives you lemons—and soaring hotel prices, higher air fares, and no choice but to cut back your vacation plans—you make lemonade. Then you decide whether your lemonade is sweet or sour.

If you can't open your mind to a staycation, you'll sabotage it from the start. But if you can appreciate what a staycation can offer, you might feel the same way as Amy in Ohio.

"We will probably stay home again next year because of the economy, and quite frankly, we like it that way," she said. "Staycations are the vacations of the future."

They're certainly part of the future, but the traditional vacation will be a big part of it, too. Jetting away on a big trip is what most people want, even if airlines will eventually add a fee for overhead bin space, airsickness bags, and every "buh-bye now" uttered by a flight attendant.

Big, splashy vacations are among the great pleasures in life. But so are the simple things, and that's why so much of a staycation's success is determined by your attitude.

If you want a staycation to work, you will make it work. If you don't want it to work, well, then it won't.

Some websites and blogs say staycations are a bad idea. They say that a staycation is not a vacation, it's recreation. You won't be able to break away from your daily routine, they say, and after a day or two, you'll be spending the day doing chores around the house and sitting at your computer, responding to e-mails from work.

Not surprisingly, the easiest place to find these views are on websites for travel agencies and travel guides. It's kind of like asking the Dolly Madison Bakery to weigh in on the health benefits of eating a twelve-pack of chocolate Zingers.

More importantly, however, is that most, if not all, of the people tearing down the stay-at-home vacation have never taken one. They just dismiss it as a stupid idea before encouraging everyone to take a "real" vacation. (Oh yes, and book it with us!)

It's true that a staycation isn't for everyone. But don't let anyone tell you how your vacation must be defined. You define it, you design it, and you enjoy it. That's what I did during my last staycation, which was probably more humble in scope than anything you'll plan. One day included a trip with my six-year-old to the indoor aquatic center in our city. It was just me and Ryan. Cooper, my three-year-old, stayed at home with my wife and the baby. Cooper later got a special "Dad and Me" day, too.

Ryan and I went to the aquatic center and swam for a few hours. He went down some slides, sprayed me with water, and showed me his swimming moves. Afterward, we stopped at a restaurant to get some cookies. We sat down to eat them, and between bites, Ryan asked me this:

"Dad, don't you think this is the best special day ever?"

That's all it took for the best special day ever. Swimming and cookies.

Obviously, it's easier to impress a six-year-old than a thirty-six-year-old. But even if you don't have kids, if you take that youthful exuberance into your staycation, it will be a great vacation. No, it won't be the vacation of a lifetime, but you've got a lifetime to take that vacation.

Just make your staycation the best vacation for this time in your life. Plan ahead, take a few risks, and keep your sense of humor. And always remember this:

You can plan for the future and still live for the now.

Good luck.

Afterword

So now we're at the end of the book . . . and possibly the start of your staycation. I wish you the best, and if you want to share your experience, you can find me at *www.mattwixon.com*. I'd love to hear how it went, what worked, what didn't, and whether you'll try it again.

Any staycation ideas you can pass along also would be great. I'm not planning *Staycation: The Sequel*, but I've got three kids and I know we'll be taking many staycations in the future. Maybe even after the economy stabilizes, the kids grow up, and a dictionary recognizes *staycation* as a word. (It's going to happen. *Wedgie* is an official word now.)

Appendix
Online Staycation Resources

Theme Park and Thrill Rides Web Resources

www.themeparkinsider.com: List and links to more than 200 U.S. theme parks, plus reviews and advice

www.sixflags.com: Six Flags, Inc. operates twenty-one theme parks and water parks in the United States and Canada

www.cedarfair.com: Cedar Fair Entertainment Co. operates seventeen theme and water parks in the United States and Canada

www.rcdb.com: Rollercoaster database searchable by location, name and design (bobsled, standup, suspended, etc.)

www.thrillnetwork.com: News, reviews, and forums about theme parks

www.themeparks.about.com/cs/waterparks: List of water parks by state, plus a slide guide

www.thewaterparkreview.com: Water park reviews categorized by state

www.racingschools.com: Links to racetracks nationwide that have racing schools

www.uspa.org: U.S. Parachute Association site lists skydiving schools throughout the country

www.bodyflight.net: Links to vertical wind tunnels in the United States *www.bungeezone.com*: Links to companies that offer bungee jumping, categorized by state

www.ababmx.com: American Bicycle Association's links to U.S. BMX tracks

www.funcenterdirectory.com: Links to family fun centers across the country

www.daveandbusters.com, *www.gameworks.com*: Entertainment centers with restaurants, games for adults and older kids

www.indoorclimbing.com: List of climbing facilities in the United States

Outdoors and Adventure Web Resources

www.dayhiker.com: Day hiker resources

www.localhikes.com: Links to local hiking trails nationwide

www.gorp.com: Hiking guides, list of trails, state-by-state list of rafting rivers

www.americantrails.org: Database of National Recreation Trails

www.offroaders.com: Links to off-roading clubs across the country

www.nps.gov: National Park Service

www.goski.com: Links to ski resorts across the country

www.wildlifeviewingareas.com: List of wildlife viewing areas in the United States

www.whalewatching.com, www.whaleguide.com: Links to whale-watching tours

www.horseandtravel.com: Contact information for riding stables across the country

www.pickyourown.org: List and description of farms that allow visitors to pick fruit

www.lovetheoutdoors.com: Camping tips, links to private and public campsites

Educational Staycation Web Resources

www.factorytoursusa.com: Links to more than 500 factory tours

www.museumnetwork.com: Listings and links to 37,000 museums, searchable by area

www.astronomyclubs.com: Links to observatories and planetariums across the country

www.classtrips.com: Links to destinations and day trips for kids

www.howtocompost.org: Composting how-to for beginners

www.berlitz.com: Links to language training centers and online classes

www.volunteermatch.org: Search your hometown for volunteer opportunities

www.genealogylinks.net: Links to genealogy resources, searchable by state

www.aza.org: Association of Zoos and Aquariums has links to member zoos

www.thegreenguide.com: National Geographic Society's info and ideas about green living

www.vpa.org: List of vintage home tours, categorized by state

The Pampered Life Web Resources

www.spafinder.com: Links to spas nationwide

www.spaindex.com: Ingredients and instructions for home spa treatments

www.healthclubs.com: Links to health clubs nationwide

www.massageenvy.com: Links to Massage Envy locations

www.massageregister.com: List of massage schools by zip code

www.beautyschoolsdirectory.com: Links to beauty schools nationwide

www.yogaalliance.com: List of yoga studios and instructors nationwide

www.resortsandlodges.com: List of world resorts, sorted by type and location

Sports Web Resources

www.minorleaguebaseball.com: Links to all levels of minor league baseball teams

www.wnba.com: Home of Women's National Basketball Association, with links to teams

www.usajuniorhockey.com: Links to all levels of junior hockey

www.arenafootball.com: Home of Arena Football League, with links to teams

www.af2.com: Home of Arena Football 2, with links to teams

www.usptafindapro.com: Links to tennis professionals who give lessons

www.pgapros.com: Links to golf professionals who give lessons

www.tennisresortsonline.com: Links to resorts offering tennis

www.kidscamps.com: List and information on sports camps for kids

www.upcomingcardshows.com: Calendar and information on upcoming sports collectibles shows

Movies, Plays, and Other Entertainment Web Resources

www.aact.org: American Association of Community Theatre, has searchable database of companies

www.foodreference.com: Links to food festivals, searchable by area or date

www.festivals.com: Searchable database of festivals

www.blockbuster.com, *www.netflix.com*: Online video-rental services

www.chucklemonkey.com: List and links to comedy clubs

www.openmikes.org: Listings for clubs with open-mike nights

www.poetryslam.com: Listings for poetry slams, with descriptions

www.cinematreasures.org: Information and links for historic movie theaters

www.rockyhorror.com: Home page for cult classic *The Rocky Horror Picture Show*

www.tonylovestina.com: Home page for long-running interactive play, *Tony n' Tina's Wedding*

Romantic Staycation Web Resources

www.4sitters.com: Nationwide babysitter-finding service (membership required)

www.sittercity.com: Nationwide babysitter-finding service (membership required)

www.seekingsitters.com: Nationwide babysitter-finding service (membership required)

www.barefootstudent.com: Listing of college students seeking babysitting work

www.bedandbreakfast.com: Links to bed and breakfast locations, searchable by city

www.traintraveling.com: Links to railroads with scenic day trips

www.lovingyou.com: Huge list of romantic ideas, including ones submitted from readers

www.allamericanwineries.com: List and contact information for U.S. wineries, organized by state

Especially for Kids Web Resources

www.discoverthis.com: Site that sells educational toys, including a fossil-dig kit

www.traintraveling.com: Links to railroads with scenic day trips

www.thomasandfriends.com: Schedule and information for Day Out with Thomas train rides

www.thelittleenginethatcould.com: Schedule and information for Little Engine That Could train rides

www.freeprintablecertificates.net: Printable award certificates for a variety of occasions

www.customink.com: Site for designing and ordering custom T-shirts

www.familycrafts.about.com: Ideas and instructions for crafts for kids

www.familyfun.com: Ideas for family-friendly activities

www.bizarrelabs.com: Instructions for easy science experiments with kids

www.ripleys.com: Links to Ripley's Believe It or Not museums

Additional Fun Web Resources

www.privatelessons.com: List of music instructors, searchable by area and specialty

www.miniatures.org: Home of National Association of Miniature Enthusiasts

www.videomaker.com: Instructions for editing home videos

www.volunteermatch.org: Helps people find volunteer opportunities close to home

www.earth.google.com: Home of Google Earth, a free service with satellite images of the world

www.maps.google.com: Home of Google Maps, a free service that includes street views of many areas

www.earthcam.com: Links to webcams around the world

www.homelink.org, www.intervacus.com, www.homeexchange.com: Membership sites with listings for vacation home exchanges

www.roadfood.com, www.chowhound.com: Reviews of restaurants around the country

www.carshownews.com: Schedules of classic car shows in the United States

www.beermapping.com: Maps and links to microbreweries in the United States

INDEX

About the Author

Matt Wixon, a writer and columnist for *The Dallas Morning News*, has been writing humor columns and features since his days at the University of Arizona. He studied journalism in college, at least on most weekdays, and graduated magna cum laude, which is Latin for "without money."

Wixon joined *The Dallas Morning News* in 1999 as a sports copy editor and began writing sports columns and features for the paper four years later. Since 2001, his "Humor Me" column has appeared in *The Dallas Morning News* and several other newspapers, as well as on a variety of Internet sites. He also shoots and edits sports videos for the paper's website.

Wixon is married and lives in the Dallas area. He and his wife, Janell, have three sons, Ryan, Cooper, and Nathan, who provide daily inspiration for writing and allow very little time to write.

His website is *www.mattwixon.com.*